Managing Gambel Oak in Southwestern Ponderosa Pine Forests:

The Status of Our Knowledge

Scott R. Abella

United States
Department
of Agriculture

Forest
Service

Rocky Mountain
Research Station

General Technical Report
RMRS-GTR-218

November 2008

Abella, Scott R. 2008. **Managing Gambel oak in southwestern ponderosa pine forests: the status of our knowledge**. Gen. Tech. Rep. RMRS-GTR-218. Fort Collins, CO: U.S. Department of Agriculture, Forest Service, Rocky Mountain Research Station. 27 p.

Abstract

Gambel oak (*Quercus gambelii*) is a key deciduous species in southwestern ponderosa pine (*Pinus ponderosa*) forests and is important for wildlife habitat, soil processes, and human values. This report (1) summarizes Gambel oak's biological characteristics and importance in ponderosa pine forests, (2) synthesizes literature on changes in tree densities and fire frequencies since Euro-American settlement in pine-oak forests, (3) suggests management prescriptions for accomplishing various oak management objectives (for example, increasing diameter growth or acorn production), and (4) provides an appendix containing 203 Gambel oak literature citations organized by subject. Nine studies that reconstructed Gambel oak density changes since settlement in the late 1800s reported that densities of small oaks have escalated, with increases ranging from 4- to more than 63-fold. A possible argument for passive oak management, that overall oak abundance has decreased, is not supported by published research. Manipulating oak growth forms is one of the main means for managing oak and ecosystem components affected by oak. Published research has classified variants of three basic oak growth forms: shrubby thickets of small stems, pole-sized clumps, and large trees. Burning and cutting constitute major prescriptions for manipulating these growth forms, whereas pine thinning has most consistently increased oak diameter growth for promoting large oaks. Because of their high ecological value, large, old oaks should be retained in any management prescription. Sufficient research has been published on which to base some oak management prescriptions, but additional research on poorly understood aspects of oak's ecology is needed to refine and improve oak management.

Key words: *Pinus ponderosa*, *Quercus gambelii*, thinning, management, ecological restoration, wildlife-habitat relationships

The Author

Scott R. Abella, at the time of writing, was Research Specialist, Sr. with the Ecological Restoration Institute at Northern Arizona University in Flagstaff, AZ. He holds a B.S. degree in Natural Resources Management from Grand Valley State University, an M.S. degree in Forest Resources from Clemson University, and a Ph.D. in Forest Science from Northern Arizona University. His present position is Assistant Research Professor, Public Lands Institute and School of Life Sciences, University of Nevada Las Vegas.

Acknowledgments

I thank Pete Fulé for providing age-diameter data from Camp Navajo and Grandview; Amy Waltz for providing oak density data from Mount Trumbull; Wally Covington for encouraging and supporting management-oriented literature syntheses; and Bill Kruse, J.P. Roccaforte, Judy Springer, Pete Ffolliott, Catherine Wightman, Kristi Coughlon, and Sharon Altman for reviewing the manuscript. Funding was provided by the U.S. Forest Service and the Ecological Restoration Institute. This report is dedicated to the late Bill Kruse, who did much to advance our understanding of Gambel oak ecology and whose willingness to share his knowledge with me improved the manuscript.

Contents

Cover photos by S.R. Abella, summer 2004, on the Coconino National Forest, northern AZ.

Managing Gambel Oak in Southwestern Ponderosa Pine Forests: The Status of Our Knowledge

Scott R. Abella

Introduction

Gambel oak (*Quercus gambelii*) frequently is the only deciduous tree in otherwise pure southwestern ponderosa pine (*Pinus ponderosa*) forests, adding diversity to these forests (Reynolds and others 1970, Rosenstock 1998). Gambel oak and its management are important in ponderosa pine forests because oak influences soils, understory vegetation, wildlife, and human values (Clary and Tiedemann 1992, Harper and others 1985, Klemmedson 1987). Similar to pure ponderosa pine forests, fire exclusion, wood harvesting, livestock grazing, and other factors have altered pine-Gambel oak forests since Euro-American settlement in the late 1800s (Fulé and others 1997, Madany and West 1983). These factors are thought to have resulted in declines in native plant communities, ecosystem simplification, inferior habitat for some wildlife species, and susceptibility to intense wildfires (Covington and Moore 1994, Wightman and Germaine 2006). Currently, much attention is given to managing ponderosa pine forests to reverse these deleterious changes, principally through mechanical pine thinning and prescribed burning. Less attention, however, is given to managing Gambel oak (Brischler 2002). Research published to date suggests that Gambel oak can and should be actively managed on some sites (Clary and Tiedemann 1992). Manipulating oak densities, growth forms, and diameter growth can improve wildlife habitat, understory communities, and other ecosystem values in pine-oak forests (Kruse 1992).

This report summarizes Gambel oak's biological characteristics, importance in ponderosa pine forests, evolutionary environment and changes since settlement, responses to fire and mechanical thinning, and strategies for accomplishing specific oak management objectives (for example, increasing diameter growth). This report is not intended to be an exhaustive review of oak's ecology or wildlife relationships. Readers are referred to a bibliography in the report appendix for literature detailing specific Gambel oak ecological characteristics and associations with wildlife. Focus is on summarizing our current knowledge about oak management in ponderosa pine forests to assist practitioners in developing management prescriptions and to highlight areas requiring additional research. Although many unknowns remain, sufficient published data exist on which to base some management prescriptions for Gambel oak. Testing of these prescriptions in a variety of applied management and research settings is encouraged to refine and improve the prescriptions.

Biological Characteristics

Distribution

Gambel oak occurs with ponderosa pine in Arizona, New Mexico, Colorado, Utah, and small portions of southeastern Nevada and southwestern Texas (fig. 1). Gambel oak grows primarily as an understory or mid-story tree in the southern half of its range in Arizona and New Mexico, while shorter shrub forms predominate in shrublands in the northern part of its range in Utah and Colorado (Brown 1958, Harper and others 1985).

Figure 1—Distribution of Gambel oak. Isolated populations also occur in southwestern Texas. After Clary and Tiedemann (1992), modified from Little (1971).

USDA Forest Service Gen. Tech. Rep. RMRS-GTR-218. 2008

1

The species occupies a variety of soil parent materials including basalt, benmoreite, limestone, sandstone, shale, granite, and volcanic cinders (Hanks and others 1983, Humphries and Bourgeron 2003, Muldavin and others 1990). While habitat affinities can change regionally and with elevation, Gambel oak in Arizona and New Mexico ponderosa pine forests occupies a range of aspects and topography including canyons, small drainages, flat plains, and cinder cones (Hanks and others 1983). Oak inhabits rocky and non-rocky sites (Hanks and others 1983, Neilson and Wullstein 1986).

Regeneration

Gambel oak is a clonal species and a member of the white oak group (Harper and others 1985). The species regenerates naturally from both seed and sprouts. Sopp and others (1977) reported high germination percentages for fall-collected acorns from Colorado (fig. 2). More than 90 percent of untreated acorns or acorns treated with 14 to 28 days of cool-moist stratification germinated.

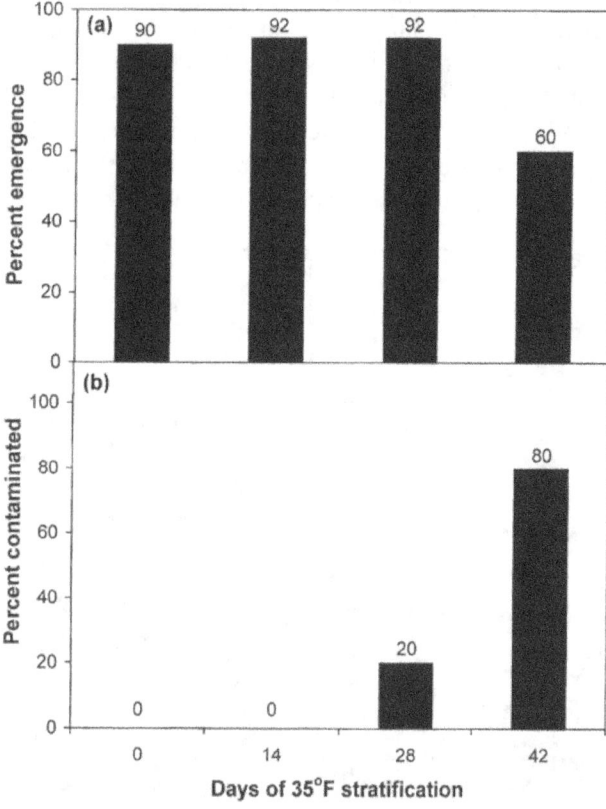

Figure 2—Emergence (≈ germination) and contamination of Gambel oak acorns collected in Colorado after various durations of cool, moist stratification. Emergence declined, while contamination (by mold and other damaging agents) increased, after 28 days of stratification. Data from Sopp and others (1977).

Oak seedling establishment from acorns appears more prevalent in pine forests than in the northern areas of oak's range where the species forms shrublands. At 15 pine-oak sites in Arizona and New Mexico, for example, Neilson and Wullstein (1986) found that oak seedling densities ranged from 49 to 534/acre (120 to 1,320/ha). These authors differentiated seedlings from sprouts by excavating roots or observing the presence or absence of spent acorns. Forty-one percent of the seedlings established on northeastern sides of sheltering objects (for example, rocks or shrubs), compared to only 14 percent on southwestern sides. These northeastern microhabitats are cooler and moister (Neilson and Wullstein 1986). In an outplanting experiment using first-year seedlings from northern Utah seed sources, short-term (< 2 years) seedling survival exceeded 50 percent at two sites in Arizona and New Mexico (Neilson and Wullstein 1983). Major sources of mortality identified by these authors included spring freezing, summer drought, and grazing. Mortality rates due to other factors (for example, fire) remain unclear for naturally established seedlings in ponderosa pine forests.

It is well documented that Gambel oak vigorously resprouts from extensive root systems after disturbances such as cutting, grazing, or intense fire kill stems (Ffolliott and Gottfried 1991, Kunzler and Harper 1980, Tiedemann and others 1987). These disturbances likely result in sharp increases in densities of small-diameter oak stems. Disturbances that are especially severe (for example, overstory clearcutting or wildfire) may result in the development of persistent oak brushfields (Ffolliott and Gottfried 1991, Savage and Mast 2005). However, it remains unclear if resprouting ability changes as oak clones age, which is important to clarify in future research (Clary and Tiedemann 1992).

Growth and Longevity

Gambel oak diameter growth is generally slow relative to ponderosa pine. Based on 134 sample trees in central Arizona, Barger and Ffolliott (1972) provided estimates of average diameter growth for oaks that ranged in diameter from 2 to 36 inches (5 to 91 cm). Average diameter growth of trees by diameter class was as follows: 2-inch (5-cm) trees = 0.062 inches/yr (0.16 cm/yr), 10-inch (25-cm) trees = 0.058 inches/yr (0.15 cm/yr), 20-inch (51-cm) trees = 0.054 inches/yr (0.14 cm/yr), and 36-inch (91-cm) trees = 0.049 inches/yr (0.12 cm/yr).

Regressions of oak diameter and age, developed from three sites in northern Arizona, indicate that diameter explained between 82 and 89 percent of the variation in age based on non-linear equations (fig. 3). Table 1 shows

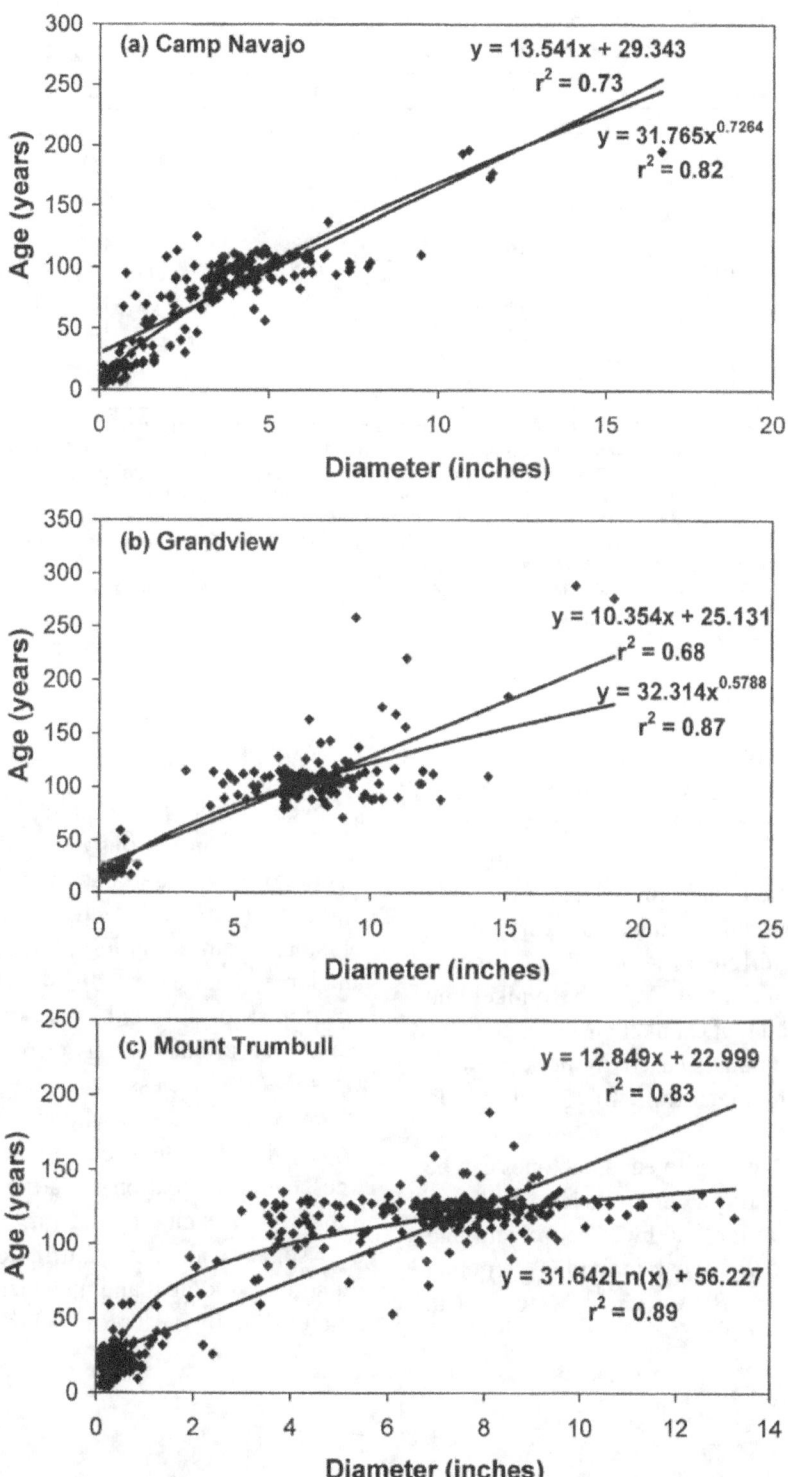

Figure 3—Relationship of age with diameter at breast height of Gambel oak at three sites in northern Arizona ponderosa pine forests. Ages do not account for time required to reach the coring height of 16 inches (40 cm), which may require more than 17 years (Neilson and Wullstein 1986). Linear equations are given along with equations exhibiting the highest r^2. Numbers of trees included in the regressions are as follows: (a) = 187, (b) = 195, and (c) = 411. Data provided by the Ecological Restoration Institute, Flagstaff, AZ, associated with the following published studies: (a) = Fulé and others (1997), (b) = Fulé and others (2005), and (c) = Waltz and others (2003).

USDA Forest Service Gen. Tech. Rep. RMRS-GTR-218. 2008

3

Table 1—Average ages of Gambel oak at different diameters at breast height (DBH) for three sites in northern Arizona ponderosa pine forests.

DBH (inches)	Camp Navajo	Grandview	Mt. Trumbull
	---------------- Age (years)[a]----------------		
2	53	46	78
4	87	67	100
6	117	87	113
8	144	108	122
10	169	129	129
12	193	149	135
14	216	170	140
16	238	191	—
18	—[b]	212	—

[a]Ages estimated using regression equations shown in fig. 3 exhibiting the highest r^2 value, with the exception of the Grandview site. A linear regression was used at this site to most accurately estimate ages of large trees. Estimated ages do not account for time required to reach the coring height of 16 inches (40 cm). Data provided by the Ecological Restoration Institute, Flagstaff, AZ, associated with the following published studies: Camp Navajo = Fulé and others (1997), Grandview = Fulé and others (2005), and Mt. Trumbull = Waltz and others (2003).

[b]Ages were not estimated beyond the largest tree in the data set for each site.

predicted ages of oaks of various diameters based on these equations. While there is variability both within and among sites, oaks greater than 10 inches (25 cm) in diameter in this area generally became established before Euro-American settlement in the late 1800s. Little is known about how oak growth rates may vary on different soil types or in different regions. In the Lincoln National Forest in southern New Mexico, Ryniker and others (2006) also found that Gambel oak diameter was correlated ($r^2 = 0.81$) with age based on measurements of 28 trees ranging in diameter from 1 to 7 inches (2 to 17 cm).

Individual stems can be long-lived, and clones can be older than the oldest existing stem. In their compilation of oldest known trees in the Southwest, Swetnam and Brown (1992) listed a Gambel oak individual stem that was 401 years old on the Beaver Creek watershed in north-central Arizona.

Growth Forms

Several authors have classified Gambel oak growth forms based on various tree and clump characteristics (table 2). These classifications have generally recognized variants of three basic growth forms: shrubby thickets of small stems, clumps of intermediate-sized stems, and large, mature trees (fig. 4). The classifications were developed for different purposes and emphasize different aspects of oak ecology (Abella 2008). For example, Kruse's (1992) classification emphasizes a perceived successional process whereby oak clumps begin as brushy thickets, then self-thin to produce large, mature trees. His classification was designed to quantify wildlife habitat, with each growth form providing unique cover, browse, mast, and cavity attributes. These growth forms illustrate ecological and management tradeoffs. For example, shrubby oaks provide browse and cover near the

Table 2—Comparison of Gambel oak growth form classifications in ponderosa pine-oak forests.

Kruse 1992	Rosenstock 1998	Abella and Springer 2008
Successional stage	Stem diameter (inches)	Stem density, spacing
1. Brushy (youngest)	1. Shrub like (< 1)	1. Single stem
2. Young pole stand	2. Small tree (1 to 8)	2. Dispersed clump (low-high, wide)
3. Mature	3. Mature tree (8 to 15)	3. Thicket (high, close)
4. Post mature (oldest)	4. Large, old tree (> 15)	

Figure 4—Gambel oak occurs as gradations of three basic growth forms in ponderosa pine forests: (a) single trees, (b) clumps, and (c) dense thickets. These basic growth forms have been identified by various authors (table 2). Photos by S.R. Abella, summer 2004, on the Coconino National Forest, northern AZ.

ground but produce few acorns, while larger oaks supply more acorns but offer little ground-level browse or cover (Kruse 1992, McCulloch and others 1965). While not all oaks encountered in the field readily fit into a classification scheme, these existing classifications may be useful for understorying oak ecology, inventorying sites and measuring habitat quality, and developing and monitoring management treatments.

Fire Ecology

Although pine-oak forests typically historically burned more frequently than every 15 years (for example, Grissino-Mayer and others 2004), Brown and Smith (2000) report that Gambel oak has low fire resistance at maturity and at any size. According to Simonin (2000), Gambel oak bark ranges from 0.5 to 0.75 inches (1.2 to 1.9 cm) thick, categorized by Brown and Smith (2000) as "thin." No information was provided, however, as to whether bark thickness increases as oak ages. Nevertheless, large oaks may have had some capacity to survive low-intensity presettlement fires (Abella and Fulé 2008a). Rocky microsites or other areas oak sometimes occupies also may have burned less frequently than surrounding areas, but oak also occupies relatively uniform sites with few barriers to fire spread (Hanks and others 1983). Looser, less resinous, and moister oak litter (compared to pine litter) may have burned less intensively near oak boles, allowing large oaks to persevere (Abella and Fulé 2008a). In addition to some ability of large stems to survive low-intensity fire, oaks top-killed by fire often resprout (Kunzler and Harper 1980). Following Rowe's (1983) classification of plant adaptations to fire, Gambel oak is thus both a resister (by survival of some large oaks) and an endurer (by resprouting) of fire. Estimates of survival following prescribed burning and suggestions for increasing survival during burns are given in the Prescribed Burning section of the Management Objectives part of this report.

Importance in Ponderosa Pine Forests_____

Effects on Soils

Relative to ponderosa pine, increasing oak basal area coincided with increased concentrations of several nutrients (C, N, P, S, Ca, Mg, and K) in basalt soils in northern Arizona pine-oak forests (Klemmedson 1987, 1991). Oak likely enhanced nutrient concentrations relative to pine partly by producing leaves containing more concentrated

USDA Forest Service Gen. Tech. Rep. RMRS-GTR-218. 2008

5

nutrients (table 3). Nitrogen and Ca, for example, were more than twice as concentrated in oak leaves as in pine needles (Klemmedson 1987). Klemmedson (1987) also found that oak increased upper O horizon pH relative to pine but did not affect mineral soil pH. In greenhouse experiments using 0- to 6-inch (0- to 15-cm) mineral soil collected from stands with varying proportions of oak, Klemmedson (1991) found that barley (*Hordeum vulgare*) yields from soils with 50 percent oak were three times greater than those with no oak. Pine seedling biomass also was greater in soils collected from stands with high oak basal area. These studies suggest that oak is important in soil nutrient cycling, and increasing concentrations of soil nutrients can be expected with increasing oak relative to pine.

Effects on Understory Vegetation

Soil properties, light, and other environmental variables differ below Gambel oak canopies compared to below ponderosa pine or openings (Abella, In prep; Brown 1958; Madany and West 1984). Several studies have found that environments below oak support plant communities differing from those below other canopy types (Brown 1958, Evenson and others 1980, Madany and West 1984). In Colorado, for example, Brown (1958) found that elk sedge (*Carex geyeri*) biomass averaged 204 lbs/acre (229 kg/ha) below oak compared to only 25 lbs/acre (28 kg/ha) in openings. In southern Utah, Evenson and others (1980) also found that elk sedge, in addition to tuber starwort (*Pseudostellaria jamesiana*), was more abundant below oak than in openings. In northern Arizona pine-oak forests, numerous species differentiated along a tree canopy gradient including openings, three types of oak canopies, and ponderosa pine (Abella and Springer 2008; fig. 5). For example, the warm-season grass pine dropseed (*Blepharoneuron tricholepis*) occurred in openings and below single oaks, but declined in frequency below denser oak and pine canopies. Aspen pea (*Lathyrus laetivirens*), in contrast, was most frequent below dense oak thickets. These data suggest that plant community composition differs below oak compared to other canopy types and varies among oak growth forms as well.

Table 3—Chemical properties of freshly fallen ponderosa pine needles and Gambel oak leaves collected on basalt soils 25 miles (40 km) south of Flagstaff, AZ. Many nutrients were more concentrated in oak leaves than in pine needles. Data from Klemmedson (1987).

Variable	Pine	Oak
C (percent)[a]	48.7	44.6
N (percent)	.40	.97
P (percent)	.04	.19
S (percent)	.05	.08
Ca (percent)	.37	.83
Mg (percent)	.13	.35
K (percent)	.13	.46
C/N ratio	122	46
pH	3.9	4.9

[a]Percent by weight.

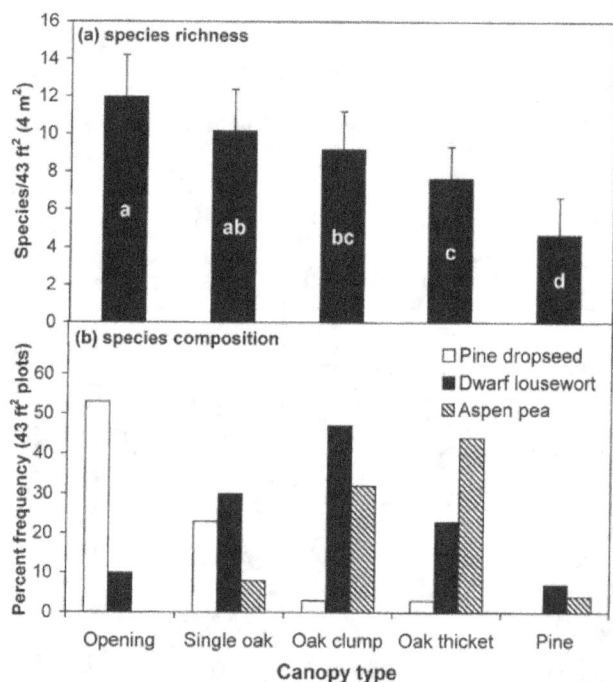

Figure 5—Comparison of plant species richness and composition in openings, below three oak canopy types, and below ponderosa pine in northern Arizona pine-oak forests. Oak canopy types exhibited intermediate species richness and were favored by species such as dwarf lousewort (*Pedicularis centranthera*). In (a), error bars are one standard deviation and letters indicate significant differences at $P < 0.05$ (one-way analysis of variance, Fisher's least significant difference for mean separation). Data from Abella and Springer (2008).

Competition With Pine

Biondi and others (1992) noted that overstory ponderosa pine do not compete with the shorter Gambel oak for light, and any competition between the species would probably be for soil moisture, nutrients, and growing space. Gambel oak's extensive root system does uptake copious moisture (Tew 1967), and oak appears more drought-tolerant than ponderosa pine (Kolb and Stone 2000). In northern Arizona pine-oak forests, Biondi and others (1992) concluded that pine-pine competition slowed pine diameter growth more than oak-pine competition. This may have resulted from oak's positive influence on soil nutrients or pine's increased spacing in the presence of oak (Biondi and others 1992). Some authors have suggested that oak and its effects on soils and microclimates may promote pine seedling establishment (Floyd 1982). Other authors have suggested the opposite because of possible allelopathic effects of oak leaves on pine germination (Harrington 1987). Several studies suggest that oak proliferation after severe disturbance, such as wildfire or clearcutting, may contribute to delays in pine reestablishment (for example, Ffolliott and Gottfried 1991, Savage and Mast 2005). However, these post-disturbance oak shrublands contribute wildlife habitat and other values (Ffolliott and Gottfried 1991). Research published to date suggests that pine-pine competition may be more intense than oak-pine competition (Biondi and others 1992); pine-oak competition may slow oak growth particularly for older stems (Onkonburi 1999); and competitive relationships between pine and oak may depend on oak growth form and age (for example, sprouts versus old stems; Tew 1967).

Wildlife Habitat

Gambel oak influences wildlife habitat by providing cover, acorns and foliage for food, feeding surfaces for insects and associated predators, cavities and surfaces for cavity excavation, and by affecting other ecosystem components such as soils, microclimates, and invertebrates (Harper and others 1985, Leidolf and others 2000, Reynolds and others 1970). In Gambel oak shrublands in Utah, for example, Hayward (1948) found that invertebrate density was six times higher in soils below oak than in open areas. In a northern Arizona study of breeding birds, Rosenstock (1998) reported that overall bird diversity and species richness of Neotropical migrants, ground nesters, primary cavity excavators, and secondary cavity users were higher in pine-oak than in pure ponderosa pine forests. Of 42 total species detected, 10, including red-faced warblers (*Cardellina rubrifrons*), house wrens (*Troglodytes aedon*), and downy woodpeckers (*Picoides pubescens*), were most common in forests containing oak (Rosenstock 1998). An important conclusion from wildlife studies is that different growth forms, diameters, and heights of oak provide different habitat for wildlife species (Kruse 1992, Lesh 1999, Rosenstock 1998). Species may respond positively, negatively, or neutrally to the presence or absence of oak, and responses for some species may change with oak growth forms (Neff and others 1979).

Human Values

Humans benefit from oak's positive effects on ecosystem components, such as wildlife habitat and soil ecology (Klemmedson 1987, Neff and others 1979). Humans also value oak aesthetically and for consumptive uses such as for fuelwood (Harper and others 1985). Gambel oak constitutes a particularly important fuelwood, with heat contents that are 24 percent greater than Utah juniper (*Juniperus osteosperma*) and 43 percent greater than ponderosa pine (Barger and Ffolliott 1972).

Evolutionary Environment

The habitat conditions in which Gambel oak evolved provide an ecological basis for management. With the exception of Madany and West's (1983) study of isolated mesas in Utah, fire-history studies have found that surface fires burned ponderosa pine-Gambel oak forests on average at least once every ≤ 13 years prior to postsettlement fire exclusion (table 4). At a northern Arizona pine-oak site, Fulé and others (1997) estimated that 40 percent of historical fires occurred in spring (late April to June) and 60 percent in summer (July to early September). Lightning is thought to have provided sufficient ignitions to support the frequent-fire regime of pine-oak forests, although human ignitions may have augmented lightning ignitions. Research published to date suggests that frequent, spring-summer fires have long been part of Gambel oak's evolutionary environment in southwestern pine-oak forests. These fires promoted open stands for both pine and oak, top-killed small stems, and stimulated resprouting (Fulé and others 1997, Waltz and others 2003).

Tree-density reconstruction studies have found that Gambel oak densities in presettlement pine-oak forests were generally less than 40 trees/acre (99/ha; table 5). However, higher densities of small sprouts may have occurred but could be difficult for contemporary reconstruction studies to detect because of decomposition.

USDA Forest Service Gen. Tech. Rep. RMRS-GTR-218. 2008

7

Table 4—Summary of surface fire frequencies before fire exclusion in ponderosa pine-Gambel oak forests. With some exceptions, pine-oak forests generally burned at least once every 10 years, similar to pure ponderosa pine forests. Compiled from Abella and Fulé (2008a).

Location	MFI (years)[a]	Reconstruction period	Elevation (feet)	Reference
Rincon Mountains, AZ	6 to 10	1657 to 1893	>7,544	Baisan and Swetnam 1990
Camp Navajo, AZ	4	1637 to 1883	7,134 to 8,046	Fulé and others 1997
Grand Canyon National Park, AZ	4	1744 to 1879	7,708	Fulé and others 2003a
Grand Canyon National Park, AZ	3 to 7	1679 to 1899	7,360 to 7,767	Fulé and others 2003b
Gila National Forest, NM	4 to 8	1633 to 1900	7,639 to 8,397	Swetnam and Dieterich 1985
San Juan National Forest, CO	7 to 13	1679 to 1880	7,380 to 8,397	Grissino-Mayer and others 2004
Zion National Park, UT – Plateau[b]	4 to 7	Pre-1881	6,429 to 7,888	Madany and West 1983
Zion National Park, UT – Mesa[b]	56 to 79	1757 to 1980	7,052 to 7,393	Madany and West 1983

[a]Range of mean fire return intervals.
[b]This study included 8,994-acre (3,640-ha) plateau and 371-acre (150-ha) isolated mesa study sites.

Table 5—Summary of studies measuring changes in oak and pine densities in ponderosa pine-Gambel oak forests. All studies found that densities of both oak and pine have sharply increased since Euro-American settlement in the late 1800s. Compiled from Abella and Fulé (2008b).

Location	Gambel oak		Ponderosa pine		Pre year[b]	Reference[c]
	Pre[a]	Post[a]	Pre	Post		
	Trees/acre[d]					
Beaver Creek Watershed, N. AZ	1	63	17	769	1867	Covington and Moore 1994
Walnut Canyon, N. AZ	6	44	22	102	1876	Menzel and Covington 1997
Camp Navajo, N. AZ	34	191	26	291	1883	Fulé and others 1997
Kaibab National Forest, N. AZ	6 to 28	64 to 177	18 to 43	167 to 1,353	1887	Fulé and others 2002a
Grand Canyon National Park, N. AZ	1 to 29	32 to 264	26 to 63	78 to 261	1879, 1887	Fulé and others 2002b
Zion National Park, UT-pine/oak	0	2 to 104	1 to 23	16 to 102	1883	Madany and West 1983
Zion National Park, UT-oak woodland	31 to 115	459 to 565	0 to 1	0 to 48	1883	Madany and West 1983
Mt. Trumbull, N. AZ	17 to 30	75 to 127	13 to 171	73 to 276	1870	Roccaforte 2005
Mt. Trumbull, N. AZ	1 to 35	17 to 244	6 to 26	110 to 684	1870	Waltz and others 2003

[a]Pre = presettlement; post = postsettlement.
[b]Year for which presettlement densities were reconstructed, normally the last year in which surface fire occurred. Postsettlement measurements were made a few years before a study's publication date.
[c]An additional study, Ruess (1995), provided graphical data consistent with results of studies summarized in the table.
[d]Range of means averaged on a site basis for studies reporting results for multiple sites.

Forest reconstruction methods have been found to be reliable to within 10 percent for ponderosa pine tree density (Moore and others 2004), but accuracy is less well-known for Gambel oak. However, in a study of the longevity of oak fence posts (90 percent of which were less than 7 inches [18 cm] in diameter), Long (1941) found that oak posts could persist for more than 60 years (the oldest posts examined).

Current Conditions

Nine tree density reconstruction studies in pine-oak forests found that overall Gambel oak densities have sharply increased since fire exclusion and Euro-American settlement in the late 1800s (table 5). These increases primarily result from increases in small- and medium-sized stems (fig. 6). Oak density increases parallel widely observed increases in ponderosa pine densities (Abella

8

USDA Forest Service Gen. Tech. Rep. RMRS-GTR-218. 2008

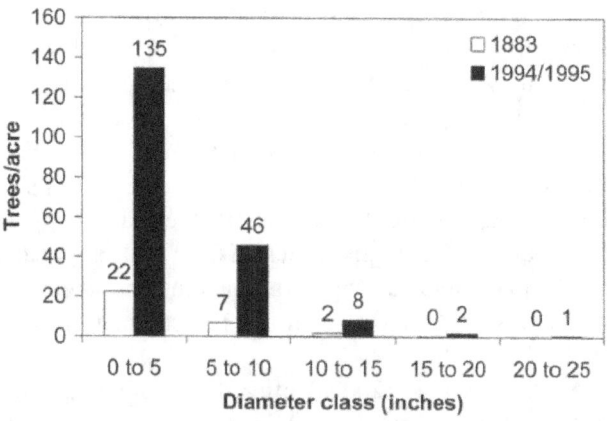

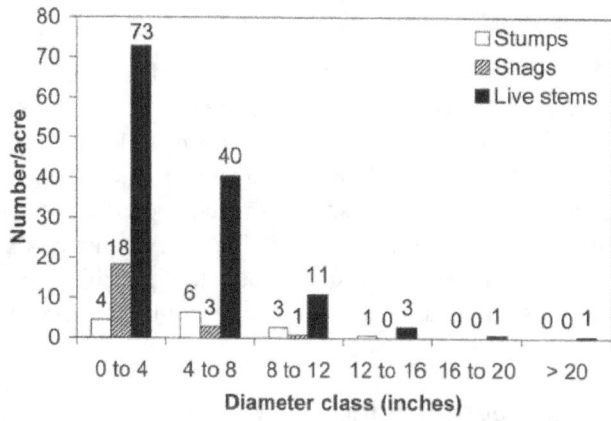

Figure 6—Gambel oak diameter distributions in 1883 and 1994/1995 in ponderosa pine-oak forests at Camp Navajo Army Depot, northern AZ. Similar to ponderosa pine, densities of small-diameter oaks have sharply increased since 1883. Data from Fulé and others (1997) and P.Z. Fulé (unpublished data).

Figure 7—Diameter distributions of standing Gambel oak stems and cut stumps measured in 2000 averaged for seven ponderosa pine-oak stands, Coconino National Forest, AZ. Data from Brischler (2002).

and Fulé 2008b, Covington and Moore 1994, Fulé and others 1997). The data are not consistent with suggestions in Rosenstock (1998) that oak abundance has declined since settlement. The increase in density that oak has exhibited is a common response in woody species following exclusion of fire (Van Auken 2000). Harper and others (1985) also noted that tolerance to defoliation and relatively low palatability for livestock may partly explain why oak has increased in abundance in many parts of its range in the past century.

It is less clear whether densities of large oaks have decreased because of fuelwood harvest or other factors. Diameter distributions in a northern Arizona pine-oak forest, however, suggest that densities of oaks greater than 10 inches (25 cm) in diameter have actually increased slightly since 1883 (fig. 6). In seven stands on the Coconino National Forest in northern Arizona, Brischler (2002) found that oak stump densities averaged 13/acre (33/ha). However, more than 70 percent of these stumps were less than 8 inches (20 cm) in diameter, consistent with the high proportion of live stems and snags in these size classes (fig. 7). Brischler (2002) hypothesized that harvesting was greater for small- to medium-sized (4- to 8-inch [10- to 20-cm] diameter) oaks than for large oaks, possibly because smaller oaks were more available, easier to cut and remove, less likely to be hollow from heart rot, or less apt to be noticed after unauthorized cutting. Branches may be more commonly cut from especially large oaks than the main stems themselves (S.R. Abella, *personal observation*). Nevertheless, past oak cutting varied

across the landscape, making generalizations difficult about possible reductions in large oaks (Brischler 2002). Evidence has not been published to date, though, that indicates that densities of large oaks on average have decreased, certainly not to the extent that densities of large ponderosa pine have diminished due to harvesting (Covington and Moore 1994). However, consideration should be given to conserving existing large oaks because of their high ecological value and old age (Harper and others 1985, Reynolds and others 1970).

In addition to small-diameter oak density increases, surface fires have been excluded from most pine-oak forests since settlement (Baisan and Swetnam 1990, Fulé and others 2003b, Grissino-Mayer and others 2004). Fire exclusion has contributed to fuel buildups and also possibly to understory compositional changes (Laughlin and others 2005). Large, old oaks may be experiencing intense competition from younger, postsettlement stems of both pine and oak. Such competition slows growth and accelerates mortality of old ponderosa pine (Wallin and others 2004) and may have similar effects on old oaks. Grazing patterns on oak also may have changed, although specifics have not been studied. In summary, oak exists in a current environment much different from the species' evolutionary environment of open stands and frequent fire. There is no general ecological basis for not actively managing oak and pine-oak sites to initiate trajectories to within a range of variability characterizing oak's evolutionary environment. Specific management objectives, however, may make passive management most appropriate and practical on many sites.

USDA Forest Service Gen. Tech. Rep. RMRS-GTR-218. 2008

9

Management Objectives _____

The following sections provide summaries of our current knowledge of suggested prescriptions for accomplishing specific oak management objectives. It is important to first define management objectives, or desired future conditions, and match prescriptions to those objectives or desired conditions. A holistic oak management strategy could include multiple objectives and prescriptions, recognizing ecosystem-level tradeoffs of various prescriptions.

Prescribed Burning

Prescribed burning can be used to manipulate oak directly (for example, to change stem density) or to meet other management objectives, such as fuel reduction. Using data from two northern Arizona pine-oak sites (Fulé and others 2005, Roccaforte 2005), Abella and Fulé (2008a) found that oak survival was diameter-specific 5 years after fall or spring prescribed burning (fig. 8). Survival of oaks greater than 6 inches (15 cm)

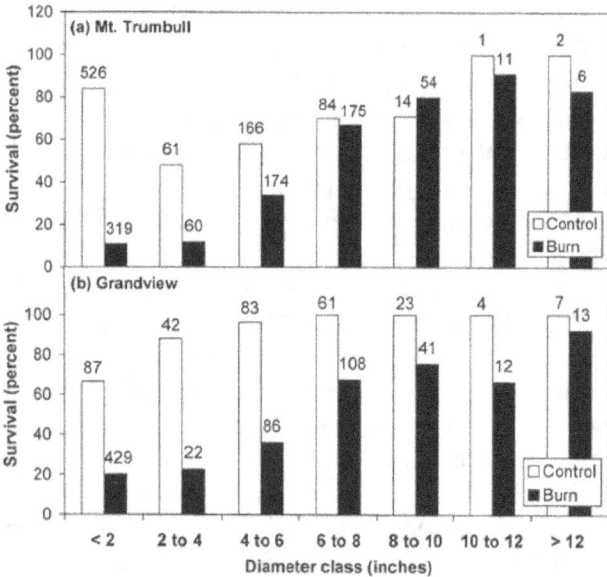

Figure 8—Survival of different sized Gambel oak stems 5 years after prescribed burning at two northern Arizona sites in ponderosa pine-oak forests. Survival exceeded 66 percent for stems greater than 6 inches (15 cm) in diameter, while survival was low for smaller stems. Numbers at the top of each bar represent the actual number of stems in each category. The (a) Mt. Trumbull study site is on the Arizona strip and managed by the Bureau of Land Management (Roccaforte 2005) and the (b) Grandview site is near the south rim of the Grand Canyon in the Kaibab National Forest (Fulé and others 2005).

in diameter exceeded 66 percent at both sites, while survival was low (11 to 20 percent) for small stems less than 2 inches (5 cm) in diameter. Survival may vary depending on operational aspects of burns, such as burn timing or whether oak clumps are deliberately lit (Ken Moore, Bureau of Land Management, personal communication 2005). Nonetheless, these data support the findings of Fulé and others (2005) that large oaks can be maintained during burns and are consistent with oak's persistence in frequent-fire presettlement forests (table 4).

Abella and Fulé (2008a) offered the following suggestions for helping to maintain large oaks during prescribed burning: (1) reduce fire intensity near oak boles or avoid deliberately lighting near oaks, (2) keep pine slash away from oaks to be retained, and (3) rake excessive fuel (particularly pine litter) away from the bases of oak boles. Contemporary fuel loads are greater than in pre-fire exclusion pine-oak forests, so raking fuel is a conservative measure that may increase oak survival. Effects of raking have not been measured, however.

Timing and frequency of burning can influence oak's resprouting ability as well as competition from other species. Harrington (1985, 1989) examined effects of burn timing (June, August, or October) and frequency (one or two burns in a 4-year period) on Gambel oak in a Colorado pine-oak stand. He found that after 4 years, all burn treatments increased densities of sprouts relative to unburned controls because of prolific sprouting of top-killed, small-diameter stems. A second burn in summer, however, resulted in the least sprouting because oak carbohydrate reserves to incite sprouting were lowest at that time. Nevertheless, burning in any season appears to kill small stems and stimulate shrub-like sprouting (Harrington 1985).

Increase Diameter Growth

Increasing oak growth rates may be an objective to encourage development of large oaks for wildlife and other values. By retrospectively examining seven pine-oak sites in northern Arizona that had been previously treated, Onkonburi (1999) found that ponderosa pine thinning resulted in the largest increase in oak diameter growth compared to oak thinning or prescribed burning (fig. 9). In an ecological restoration experiment near the south rim of the Grand Canyon, oak diameter growth also tended to be greater in areas where pine had been thinned relative to burn-only and control treatments (Fulé and others 2005). Increases in oak growth after pine thinning may be proportional to oak size or age and also to the

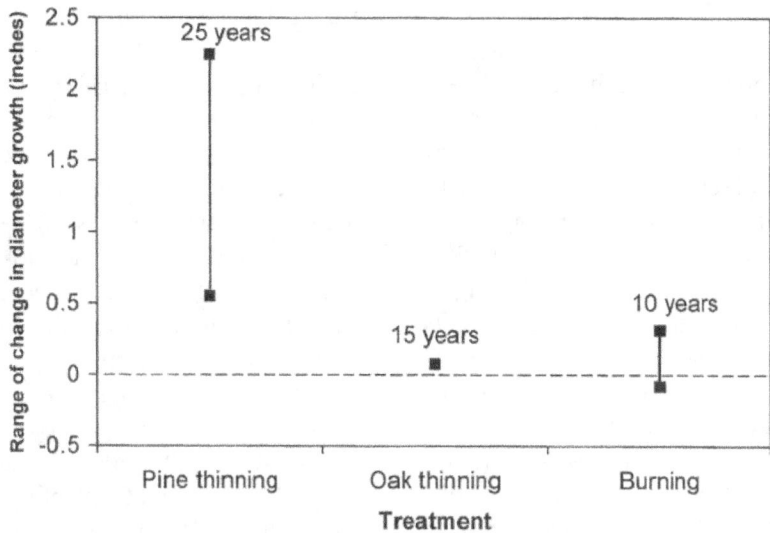

Figure 9—Reponses of Gambel oak diameter growth to mechanically thinning ponderosa pine, thinning oak within clumps, and prescribed burning measured retrospectively in northern Arizona ponderosa pine forests by Onkonburi (1999). Ranges reflect site means, except for the oak thinning treatment that included only one site. Years indicate how long growth changes persisted after treatment. Values are the total change in diameter growth during the time period.

amount of pine basal area removed, but these relationships have not been quantified. Variable and sometimes reduced oak growth after prescribed burning found by Onkonburi (1999) and Fulé and others (2005) could result from damage sustained during burns, energy allocation to resprouting rather than to growth of residual stems, or other factors.

Mechanically thinning oaks from below within oak clumps produced a slight increase in growth of large residual oaks (> 4 inches [10 cm] in diameter), but Onkonburi (1999) cautioned that findings were based on only one site and require more extensive testing (fig. 9). Accurately predicting effects of mechanically thinning oak clumps is difficult for a clonal, resprouting species like Gambel oak because responses of residual stems may depend on energy allocated to resprouting, age of the clone at the time of thinning, thinning intensity, or other factors (Clary and Tiedemann 1986, Lowell and others 1989, Touchan and Ffolliott 1999). Onkonburi's (1999) Gambel oak thinning study and data from oaks in other regions (for example, Lowell and others 1989, Shipek and others 2004) suggest that thinning oak clumps will not reduce growth of residual stems, but gains in diameter increment may not be large.

In summary, pine thinning likely produces the largest and most persistent enhancement of oak diameter growth compared to oak thinning or prescribed burning (Biondi and others 1992, Fulé and others 2005, Onkonburi 1999). Nitrogen fertilization often increases ponderosa pine growth (Youngberg 1975), but has not been tested with Gambel oak and it remains unclear if any gains would be worth the expenditure. More clearly articulating effects of pine and oak thinning, prescribed burning, and other treatments (for example, fertilization) on oak diameter growth is a key research need.

Change Density

Decreasing densities of small oak stems might be desired to return currently elevated oak densities to within an approximate range of historical variability (table 5) or to manipulate proportions of oak's growth forms (table 2, fig. 4). Burning or oak thinning can reduce oak densities, but reductions will probably only be temporary because of oak's prolific resprouting ability (Harrington 1985). Burning may be most useful for top-killing small stems less than about 6 inches in diameter (fig. 8), with summer burns resulting in the least resprouting (Harrington 1985).

USDA Forest Service Gen. Tech. Rep. RMRS-GTR-218. 2008

11

Intense burns are probably needed to reduce densities of larger stems, but more commonly, management strategies seek to maintain existing large, old oaks because of their ecological value. Based on Kruse's (1992) successional model, existing oak thickets may also self-thin through time (Clary and Tiedemann 1986). Other treatments, such as herbicides, chaining, girdling, and goat grazing, have been tested for removing oaks to increase forage primarily in Gambel oak shrublands in Colorado and Utah (Engle and others 1983). These treatments often have had mixed success in both the short and the long term (Engle and others 1983). Eliminating oak is not part of ecosystem management strategies in pine-oak forests.

Reducing competing species, such as pine, may increase oak densities (Ffolliott and Gottfried 1991). If applied infrequently, some of the same treatments (for example, prescribed burning) that initially reduce oak densities may increase densities over longer time periods (Harrington 1985). Persistence of these increases may depend on treatment frequency and self-thinning rates within oak clumps (Clary and Tiedemann 1986).

Establish New Individuals

Neilson and Wullstein (1986) found that natural seedling establishment was reasonably prevalent in Arizona and New Mexico pine-oak forests, with oak seedling densities ranging from 49 to 534/acre (120 to 1,320/ha) at 15 study sites. Methods potentially useful for establishing new oak individuals, as opposed to manipulating densities within existing clones, may include increasing seedling establishment, enhancing acorn production, and directly planting acorns or seedlings.

Oak seedling establishment may be enhanced by thinning competing trees (Ffolliott and Gottfried 1991), protecting seedlings from grazing using cages or other treatments (Neilson and Wullstein 1983), and possibly by strategically locating slash or other material near mature oaks to provide favorable microsites for acorn germination (Neilson and Wullstein 1986). On sites planned to be burned, however, slash should not be located too close to mature oaks to cause fire-related mortality. As discussed in the next section, acorn production may be increased by enhancing oak crown vigor and managing for oaks that yield the most acorns. With the exception of Neilson and Wullstein (1983), who used northern Utah seed sources from oak shrublands, little information is available about the feasibility of directly planting acorns or seedlings in ponderosa pine forests.

Increase Acorn Production

Increasing acorn production for wildlife and for enhancing natural oak regeneration may be management objectives on some sites. McCulloch and others (1965) studied acorn production of 94 Gambel oaks for 6 years on the Beaver Creek watersheds in northern Arizona. Oaks 10 to 15 inches (25 to 38 cm) in diameter, with 80 to 100 percent live crown, yielded the most acorns (fig. 10). Oaks less than 5 inches (13 cm) or greater than 18 inches (46 cm) in diameter produced few acorns. Management strategies, such as pine thinning, that promote large oaks with vigorous crowns likely will increase acorn production. However, McCulloch and others (1965) reported cyclic acorn production, with some years of no production, so periodicity of acorn crops should be expected.

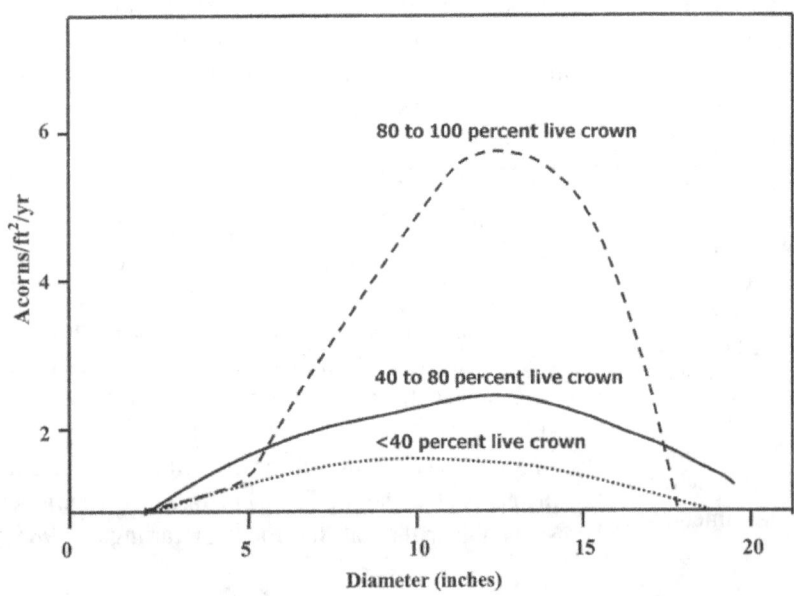

Figure 10—Gambel oak acorn production as a function of stem diameter and crown vigor, measured for 6 years on the Coconino National Forest, northern AZ. Oaks 10 to 15 inches (25 to 38 cm) in diameter and possessing 80 to 100 percent live crown yielded the most acorns. Data from McCulloch and others (1965).

Maintain or Enhance Wildlife Habitat

Different growth forms, sizes, and densities of Gambel oak provide food and habitat for different wildlife species (Leidolf and others 2000, Reynolds and others 1970). In northern Arizona pine-oak forests, for example, Lesh (1999) found that Virginia's warblers (*Vermivora virginiae*) preferentially foraged in areas containing two to three times greater oak densities than were preferred by six other bird species (fig. 11). Virginia's warblers also on average preferred oak clumps exceeding 1,500 ft^2 (139 m^2) in area, which were primarily shrub thickets dominated by small-diameter stems. Other bird species were not closely associated with this shrub-thicket growth form. Acorn production-growth form relationships illustrate another tradeoff. Small, shrubby oaks generate few acorns (McCulloch and others 1965), yet offer accessible browse and cover near the ground. In contrast, larger oaks can produce abundant acorns, but provide little ground cover or browse. Hollowness and cavity presence also are positively correlated with oak diameter (Brischler 2002, Ganey and Vojta 2004). Large, old oaks are most frequently hollow (due to heart rot) and contain the most cavities and dead wood. In northern Arizona, Brischler (2002), for instance, found that less than 8 percent of oaks less than 6 inches (15 cm) in diameter were hollow, whereas more than 64 percent of oaks greater than 14 inches (36 cm) in diameter were hollow.

Manipulating oak growth forms (table 2, fig. 4) is a key tool for managing wildlife habitat (Abella 2008). Management prescriptions for promoting different oak growth forms are summarized in table 6. Large oaks likely can be promoted by thinning competing trees, while small, shrubby forms can be maintained by fire, cutting, or other disturbances that stimulate sprouting.

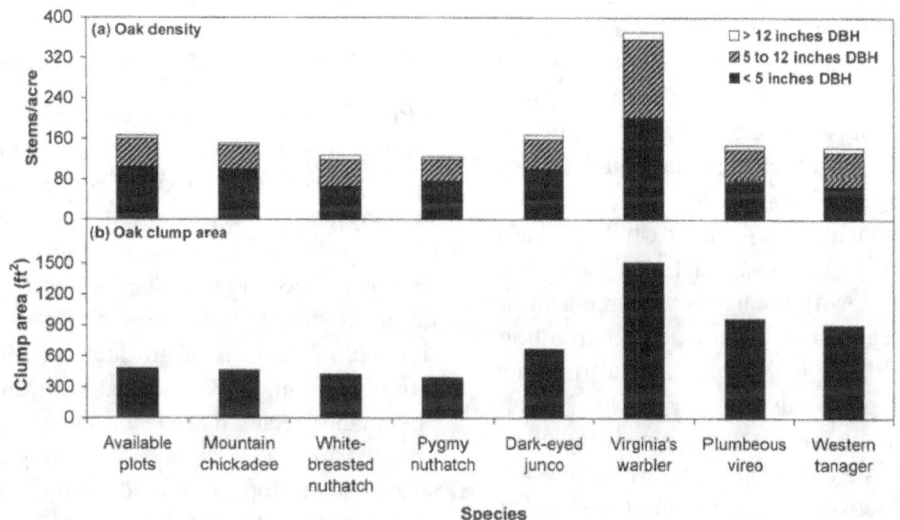

Figure 11—Gambel oak characteristics of foraging areas at a 0.01-acre (0.04-ha) plot scale for seven breeding bird species in ponderosa pine-oak forests at Camp Navajo, northern AZ. Available plots represent average conditions in the study area. Virginia's warblers selected foraging areas containing greater oak densities and clump areas than other bird species and as compared to available plots. Data from Lesh (1999).

Table 6—Summary of possible management prescriptions for promoting three basic growth forms of Gambel oak in ponderosa pine-oak forests.

Growth form	Prescriptions[a]
Large tree	Thin ponderosa pine; possibly thin within oak clumps[b]; protect large stems from damage
Pole/dispersed clump	Allow possible natural self-thinning; thin dense clumps then possibly burn; fuelwood management[c]
Brushy thicket	Burn and cut stems to facilitate sprouting; fuelwood management

[a]Prescriptions summarized primarily from Abella (2008), Abella and Fulé (2008b), Brischler (2002), Clary and Tiedemann (1992), Harrington (1989), and Onkonburi (1999). The magnitudes of the effects of the suggested prescriptions may vary with site conditions and prescription implementation. Additional research is needed to quantify effects of these variables.
[b]A particularly important area for future research is to more clearly elucidate effects of oak thinning on the growth of remaining stems.
[c]Fuelwood harvests should be carefully planned or regulated to ensure that only prescribed stem diameters and densities are cut.

USDA Forest Service Gen. Tech. Rep. RMRS-GTR-218. 2008

13

For holistic ecosystem management of wildlife communities as wholes, oak management strategies may include the following: (1) conserving all existing large, old oaks (Ganey and Vojta 2004); (2) maintaining a variety of oak growth forms including shrub-thicket forms (Rosenstock 1998); (3) being willing to cut and burn small- and medium-sized oaks to promote growth-form diversity where desired (Abella 2008); and (4) managing oak within an ecosystem context that includes treatments promoting vigorous plant communities, healthy soil processes, and overstory tree structures reasonably consistent with evolutionary environments of pine-oak forest wildlife communities (Neff and others 1979).

Although community- and ecosystem-level perspectives are often desirable, managers may need to meet single-species mandates. One example in pine-oak forests is the Mexican spotted owl (*Strix occidentalis lucida*), a threatened species under the U.S. Endangered Species Act (Prather and others 2008). Several authors have noted the importance (for example, for nest and roost sites) of Gambel oak to owls in ponderosa pine forests and have recommended managing for large oaks (May and Gutiérrez 2002, Seamans and others 1999). In a study in northern Arizona, for instance, May and others (2004) suggested managing for oaks greater than 18 inches (46 cm) in diameter that ideally contained cavities. These authors also suggested a ban on all fuelwood harvest of oak (live, dead, and down), noting that enforcement of fuelwood harvest regulations (such as only permitting removal of downed logs) is difficult. This also points to a landscape-scale perspective, a scale at which actual conflicts between single-species management and other management priorities decrease (Prather and others 2008). For example, oak fuelwood harvest could be excluded from owl habitat, while more active oak management could be performed in areas not constituting owl habitat. Care should be used to ensure, however, that passive management in owl habitat meets oak's needs as a species to maintain oak as a sustainable resource for owls and other species.

There are several potential reasons to maintain or increase current overall oak densities for wildlife habitat, even though current oak densities are orders of magnitude greater than reconstructed historical densities (table 5). For instance, it is possible that oaks provide important structural features following past logging of large ponderosa pine and current restoration thinning of small-diameter pines (May and others 2004, Wightman and Germaine 2006). Oak structure may be important for mediating the impacts to some wildlife species of rapid alteration of pine structure after thinning. There also is

less evidence that elevated densities of oak have negative ecosystem-level effects compared to high densities of ponderosa pine (for example, Allen and others 2002, Covington and Moore 1994). However, high oak density can reduce canopy openings, which are critical areas for understory plant productivity and insects constituting key resources for some wildlife species (Abella and others 2006). High oak density can also contribute to hazardous fuels, and stand-replacing wildfires destroy habitat for some wildlife species (such as owls) for long time periods (Jenness and others 2004). Elevated densities of small oaks could also interfere with the development or survival of large oak if the small stems provide competition. Another consideration is whether or not dense oak shrublands hinder pine recruitment (Savage and Mast 2005). Although maintaining elevated densities of oak may be desirable in many cases, consideration should be given to potential tradeoffs of this management strategy (Abella and others 2006).

Enhance Understory Vegetation

Plant community composition below Gambel oak canopies often differs from composition below pine and in openings (Brown 1958, Evenson and others 1980, Madany and West 1984). Different oak growth forms also support different plant communities (Abella and Springer 2008; fig. 5). Plant communities are usually the most species-rich below single oaks and the least rich below denser shrub-thickets. However, unique microenvironments associated with thickets may support plant species that are infrequent below other oak growth forms. Oak clumps containing multiple, widely spaced stems appear optimal for maintaining relatively high species richness while facilitating the coexistence of plant species requiring either open or closed-canopy environments. Pine thinning, seeding, grazing reduction, or other treatments may also be useful for enhancing understory vegetation in pine-oak forests (Clary 1975).

Browse Production

Clary (1975) listed Gambel oak as a poisonous plant for livestock on Arizona ponderosa pine ranges. Additionally, Harper and others (1988) noted that greater than 50 percent oak forage intake may cause livestock poisoning. To reduce chances of livestock poisoning when oak is a major forage species, Harper and others (1988) suggested controlling livestock intake of oak foliage until the foliage is at least 30 days old and removing livestock from oak ranges after frosts that turn leaves black. However, Harper and others (1985) concluded

14

USDA Forest Service Gen. Tech. Rep. RMRS-GTR-218. 2008

that most studies find that cattle and sheep utilize oak only after more desirable forage is diminished.

For wildlife forage, Reynolds and others (1970) noted that Gambel oak foliage comprised 8 to 77 percent of whitetail deer (*Odocoileus virginianus*), mule deer (*Odocoileus hemionus*), and elk (*Cervus canadensis*) diets in pine-oak forests. These authors also reported that browse production increases from 2- to 10-inch (5- to 25-cm) diameter oaks and declines rapidly for oaks greater than 10 inches (25 cm) in diameter. Managing for low-growing forms of oak, particularly shrub thickets, will produce the greatest amount of accessible forage.

Wood Production

Gambel oak is valued for fuelwood (Wagstaff 1984), but concerns about overharvesting have resulted in cutting restrictions in many areas (Brischler 2002). There is consensus in the literature that all large, old oaks should be retained in any management strategy (for example, Abella and Fulé 2008a, Brischler 2002, Fulé and others 2005). However, there is no support in the literature for a supposition that overall oak abundance has declined and therefore should not be actively managed anywhere on the landscape (Abella and Fulé 2008b; table 5). In fact, fuelwood harvest and cutting of young, small-diameter oaks might be useful for stimulating sprouting, manipulating oak growth forms or densities, and managing wildlife habitat and other values (Abella 2008, Clary and Tiedemann 1986, Rosenstock 1998).

Diameter-age relationships may be useful for estimating which oaks are old and therefore should not be cut. Based on data from three sites in northern Arizona pine-oak forests, probabilities are higher for oaks greater than about 6 inches (15 cm) in diameter to be considered old and of presettlement origin (fig. 3). To ensure that only prescribed oak stems are cut, any commercial or public harvests should be strictly regulated, possibly through careful marking of stems for removal. Consideration could also be given to ensuring that sufficient densities of small stems remain to grow into larger size classes to become the next cohort of old trees (Brischler 2002). Thinning oak offers an important research opportunity that may provide insight into uncertainties about Gambel oak ecology, such as whether thinning oak clumps increases growth of remaining stems (Onkonburi 1999) or if sprouting ability changes as stems or clones age (Clary and Tiedemann 1992). As emphasized in the Maintain or Enhance Wildlife Habitat section, there are many sites where cutting any oak is not appropriate for meeting management objectives.

Ecological Restoration

Ecological restoration is a management tool (Allen and others 2002, Covington and others 1997). The objective of ecological restoration is not necessarily to reestablish replicas of presettlement ecosystems, an endeavor which may be undesirable or not feasible. Instead, restoration's objective is to place degraded ecosystems on trajectories toward recovery to within a range of their historical variability (Society for Ecological Restoration International Science and Policy Working Group 2004). Managing Gambel oak using a restoration perspective may be useful in some contexts and on some sites.

Comparing reference conditions, generally agreed in pine-oak forests to be the late 1800s before Euro-American settlement (Allen and others 2002, Fulé and others 1997), to current conditions provides a basis for developing restoration prescriptions. Notable are dramatically higher densities of small-diameter trees of both oak and pine in current forests compared to reference conditions (table 5). Additionally, frequent surface fire was part of oak's evolutionary environment before fire exclusion in the late 1800s (table 4). Reducing densities of small-diameter oak and pine, principally through cutting and burning, while maintaining large, old trees, is needed to approximately reestablish presettlement conditions. For strict restoration, prescribed burning at intervals less than 10 years on most sites, preferably in summer when many fires historically occurred (Fulé and others 1997), could thin small oaks while reintroducing fire as an ecological process. Pine thinning and fuel reduction would be needed on most sites before attempting to reintroduce fire, particularly for summer burns (Allen and others 2002, Covington and others 1997).

Key Research Needs

Key research needs include refining our understanding of the effects of pine and oak thinning and prescribed burning on oak growth, as well as sharpening our knowledge of poorly understood aspects of oak ecology. Pine thinning has generally increased oak growth (Fulé and others 2005, Onkonburi 1999), but many questions remain. These questions include oak's responses to varying levels of pine thinning, whether responses change among different sizes or ages of oak, and if prescribed burning interacts with pine thinning. Uncertainties regarding oak thinning include how clones allocate energy between resprouting and growth of residual stems and whether sprouting or growth responses vary as stems or clones age (Clary and Tiedemann 1992). Prescribed burning has resulted in variable, and sometimes negative, effects on oak diameter growth (Fulé and others 2005, Onkonburi 1999). Testing effects of nearly any aspect of burning, such as timing, frequency, intensity, or implementation (for example, raking fuel away from oak boles), on oak growth and survival is an important research need as fire is reintroduced to pine-oak forests.

It is not well known whether oak diameter growth or growth forms differ with soil types or other site factors in pine-oak forests. This information would be useful for refining diameter-age relationships for identifying old trees and better predicting growth responses to management treatments. Patterns of oak seedling establishment are also poorly understood but would be important for predicting oak regeneration after disturbance and management. Another poorly understood aspect of oak ecology is the relative proportions of oak growth forms that existed in presettlement forests. Possibly this could be assessed in contemporary forests by examining how sprout densities change under different burn frequencies.

Summary and Management Implications

Biological Characteristics

- Gambel oak regenerates through both seedlings and sprouts. Prolific sprouting often occurs after stems are top-killed by cutting or fire.
- While oak growth likely varies among sites, studies at three northern Arizona sites found that stems greater than 6 to 8 inches (15 to 20 cm) in diameter are usually greater than 100 years old.
- Individual stems of Gambel oak can live for more than 400 years, and clones may live even longer.
- Gambel oak occurs in ponderosa pine-oak forests as gradations of three basic growth forms: shrubby thickets of small-diameter stems, pole-sized clumps, and large trees.
- Oak persisted in historically frequently burned forests. Preliminary information from contemporary prescribed burns suggests that some fire resistance may be attained when stem diameters exceed 6 inches (15 cm). Additional research is needed to clarify this relationship.

Importance in Ponderosa Pine Forests

- Oak adds diversity in often otherwise pure ponderosa pine forests. Oak influences soils, understory plant communities, wildlife habitat, and human values. Passive or active oak management affects these ecological properties and human values.

Evolutionary Environment

- Frequent fires and open stand conditions generally characterized oak's evolutionary environment in pine-oak forests.

Current Conditions

- Fires have been excluded and densities of both ponderosa pine and oak have increased since Euro-American settlement in the late 1800s. All nine studies examining oak density changes found that densities of small-diameter oaks have escalated, ranging from average increases of 16 to 450 stems/acre (40 to 1,112 stems/ha).
- Current conditions in pine-oak forests are outside a range of variability characterizing their evolutionary environment. There is no general ecological basis for not actively managing oak and sites containing oak, although specific objectives may require passive management.

Management Objectives

Prescribed burning

- Fire may be used to manipulate oak growth forms and stem densities, stimulate sprouting, and accomplish other management objectives (for example, fuel reduction). Preliminary evidence from three northern Arizona sites suggests that mortality will be heavy (> 60 percent) for oak stems less than 6 inches (15 cm) in diameter, but mortality decreases for larger stems.
- Several tactics may help enhance survival of ecologically valuable large oaks during prescribed fire: keeping pine slash away from oak boles, avoiding lighting near oaks or reducing fire intensity near oaks, and raking fuels away from oak clumps.

Increase diameter growth

- Thinning ponderosa pine or other competing trees will likely increase oak diameter growth. Prescribed burning has exhibited variable effects on oak growth. Mechanically thinning oak within clumps will probably not reduce growth of remaining stems, but responses are unclear because of uncertainties about energy allocation to resprouting within clones.

16

USDA Forest Service Gen. Tech. Rep. RMRS-GTR-218. 2008

Change density

- Burning and thinning oak can temporarily reduce densities, but these treatments may result in longer term increases because of oak's prolific sprouting ability.

Establish new individuals

- Oak seedling establishment may be enhanced by providing sheltered microsites (for example, strategically scattering slash), increasing acorn production, or protecting seedlings from grazing. Directly planting acorns or seedlings may also be effective, but its feasibility has not been studied.

Increase acorn production

- Oaks 10 to 15 inches (25 to 38 cm) in diameter containing vigorous crowns produced the most acorns in a northern Arizona study. Improving oak vigor, possibly through pine thinning, may boost acorn production.

Maintain or enhance wildlife habitat

- Different oak growth forms, sizes, and densities provide habitat for different wildlife species. An oak management plan for benefiting the wildlife community as a whole could entail: (1) conserving existing large, old oaks; (2) maintaining multiple oak growth forms ranging from shrubby thickets to large trees; and (3) burning or cutting small oaks to stimulate sprouting and growth-form variation where desired.

Enhance understory vegetation

- An intermediate oak growth form, consisting of clumps of widely spaced stems, optimizes understory species richness and habitat for plant species associated with oak.

Browse production

- Stimulating sprouting and managing for low-growing shrubby forms of oak will likely produce the greatest and most accessible amount of browse.

Wood production

- Cutting live oak stems would represent a policy shift in many areas. However, cutting small- and medium-sized stems, which have sharply increased since the late 1800s, has potential in specific areas for managing wildlife habitat and accomplishing other oak management objectives. Harvests should be strictly regulated to ensure that large, old oaks are not cut and sufficient stems remain to grow into large size classes.

Ecological restoration

- While not seeking to replicate presettlement conditions, densities of small-diameter oaks should be reduced and surface fire eventually reestablished for restoring oak to within a range of historical variability.
- In pine-oak forests, it could be argued that it makes little ecological sense, as a general rule, to perform restoration treatments on ponderosa pine while taking a "hands-off" approach with oak. Since oak expands after disturbances (including thinning) that reduce pine, passive oak management may have an unintended consequence of misbalancing pine and oak abundance. Additionally, a "hands-off" approach may remove flexibility from restoration prescriptions that otherwise could manipulate oak growth forms to positively restore wildlife habitat and other ecosystem values.
- On the other hand, elevated oak density could constitute key intermediary tree structure for wildlife precisely because restoration pine thinning removes large densities of small pine trees and time is required to reestablish large-tree pine structure.

References

Abella, Scott R.; Fulé, Peter Z.; Covington, W. Wallace. 2006. Diameter caps for thinning southwestern ponderosa pine forests: viewpoints, effects, and tradeoffs. Journal of Forestry. 104:407-414.

Abella, Scott R. 2008. Gambel oak growth forms: management opportunities for increasing ecosystem diversity. Res. Note RMRS-RN-37. Fort Collins, CO: U.S. Department of Agriculture, Forest Service, Rocky Mountain Research Station. 6 p.

Abella, Scott R. In prep. Tree canopy types constrain plant distributions in ponderosa pine-Gambel oak forests, northern Arizona. Res. Note RMRS-RN-##. Fort Collins, CO: U.S. Department of Agriculture, Forest Service, Rocky Mountain Research Station.

Abella, Scott R.; Fulé, Peter Z. 2008a. Fire effects on Gambel oak in southwestern ponderosa pine-oak forests. Res. Note RMRS-RN-34. Fort Collins, CO: U.S. Department of Agriculture, Forest Service, Rocky Mountain Research Station. 6 p.

Abella, Scott R.; Fulé, Peter Z. 2008b. Changes in Gambel oak densities in southwestern ponderosa pine forests since Euro-American settlement. Res. Note RMRS-RN-36. Fort Collins, CO: U.S. Department of Agriculture, Forest Service, Rocky Mountain Research Station. 6 p.

Abella, Scott R.; Springer, Judith D. 2008. Canopy-tree influences along a soil parent material gradient in Pinus-ponderosa-Quercus gambelii forests, northern Arizona. Journal of the Torrey Botanical Society. 135:26-36.

Allen, Craig D.; Savage, Melissa; Falk, Donald A.; Suckling, Kieran F.; Swetnam, Thomas W.; Shulke, Todd; Stacey, Peter B.; Morgan, Penelope; Hoffman, Martos; Klingel, Jon T. 2002. Ecological restoration of southwestern ponderosa pine forests: a broad perspective. Ecological Applications. 12:1418-1433.

Baisan, Christopher H.; Swetnam, Thomas W. 1990. Fire history on a desert mountain range: Rincon Mountain Wilderness, Arizona, U.S.A. Canadian Journal of Forest Research. 20:1559-1569.

USDA Forest Service Gen. Tech. Rep. RMRS-GTR-218. 2008

17

Barger, Roland L.; Ffolliott, Peter F. 1972. Physical characteristics and utilization of major woodland tree species in Arizona. Res. Pap. RM-83. Fort Collins, CO: U.S. Department of Agriculture, Forest Service, Rocky Mountain Forest and Range Experiment Station. 80 p.

Biondi, Franco; Klemmedson, James O.; Kuehl, Robert O. 1992. Dendrochronological analysis of single-tree interactions in mixed pine-oak stands of central Arizona, USA. Forest Ecology and Management. 48:321-333.

Brischler, Erik J. 2002. Size structure and spatial arrangement of Gambel oak in northern Arizona. Flagstaff, AZ: Northern Arizona University. 128 p. Thesis.

Brown, Harry E. 1958. Gambel oak in west-central Colorado. Ecology. 39:317-327.

Brown, James K.; Smith, Jane Kapler, eds. 2000. Wildland fire in ecosystems: effects of fire on flora. Gen. Tech. Rep. RMRS-GTR-42-vol. 2. Ogden, UT: U.S. Department of Agriculture, Forest Service, Rocky Mountain Research Station. 257 p.

Clary, Warren P. 1975. Range management and its ecological basis in the ponderosa pine type of Arizona: the status of our knowledge. Res. Pap. RM-158. Fort Collins, CO: U.S. Department of Agriculture, Forest Service, Rocky Mountain Forest and Range Experiment Station. 35 p.

Clary, Warren P.; Tiedemann, Arthur R. 1986. Distribution of biomass within small tree and shrub form *Quercus gambelii* stands. Forest Science. 32:234-242.

Clary, Warren P.; Tiedemann, Arthur R. 1992. Ecology and values of Gambel oak woodlands. In: Ffolliott, Peter F.; Gottfried, Gerald J.; Bennett, Duane A.; Hernandez, C., Victor Manuel; Ortega-Rubio, Alfredo; Hamre, R.H., tech. coords. Ecology and management of oaks and associated woodlands: perspectives in the southwestern United States and northern Mexico; 1992 April 27-30; Sierra Vista, AZ. Gen. Tech. Rep. RM-218. Fort Collins, CO: U.S. Department of Agriculture, Forest Service, Rocky Mountain Forest and Range Experiment Station: 87-95.

Covington, W. Wallace; Fule, Peter Z.; Moore, Margaret M.; Hart, Stephen C.; Kolb, Thomas E.; Mast, Joy N.; Sackett, Stephen S.; Wagner, Michael R. 1997. Restoring ecosystem health in ponderosa pine forests of the Southwest. Journal of Forestry. 95:23-29.

Covington, W. Wallace; Moore, Margaret M. 1994. Southwestern ponderosa forest structure: changes since Euro-American settlement. Journal of Forestry. 92:39-47.

Engle, D.M.; Bonham, C.D.; Bartel, L.E. 1983. Ecological characteristics and control of Gambel oak. Journal of Range Management. 36:363-365.

Evenson, William E.; Brotherson, Jack D.; Wilcox, Richard B. 1980. Relationship between environmental and vegetational parameters for understory and open-area communities. Great Basin Naturalist. 40:167-174.

Ffolliott, Peter F.; Gottfried, Gerald J. 1991. Natural tree regeneration after clearcutting in Arizona's ponderosa pine forests: two long-term case studies. Res. Note RM-507. Fort Collins, CO: U.S. Department of Agriculture, Forest Service, Rocky Mountain Forest and Range Experiment Station. 6 p.

Floyd, Mary E. 1982. The interaction of piñon pine and Gambel oak in plant succession near Dolores, Colorado. Southwestern Naturalist. 27:143-147.

Fulé, Peter Z.; Covington, W. Wallace; Moore, Margaret M. 1997. Determining reference conditions for ecosystem management of southwestern ponderosa pine forests. Ecological Applications. 7:895-908.

Fulé, Peter Z.; Covington, W. Wallace; Moore, Margaret M.; Heinlein, Thomas A.; Waltz, Amy E.M. 2002a. Natural variability in forests of the Grand Canyon, USA. Journal of Biogeography. 29:31-47.

Fulé, Peter Z.; Covington, W. Wallace; Smith, H.B.; Springer, Judith D.; Heinlein, Thomas A.; Huisinga, Kristin D.; Moore, Margaret M. 2002b. Comparing ecological restoration alternatives: Grand Canyon, Arizona. Forest Ecology and Management. 170:19-41.

Fulé, Peter Z.; Crouse, Joseph E.; Heinlein, Thomas A.; Moore, Margaret M.; Covington, W. Wallace; Verkamp, Greg. 2003a. Mixed-severity fire regime in a high-elevation forest: Grand Canyon, Arizona. Landscape Ecology. 18:465-486.

Fulé, Peter Z.; Heinlein, Thomas A.; Covington, W. Wallace; Moore, Margaret M. 2003b. Assessing fire regimes on Grand Canyon landscapes with fire scar and fire record data. International Journal of Wildland Fire. 12:129-145.

Fulé, Peter Z.; Laughlin, Daniel C.; Covington, W. Wallace. 2005. Pine-oak forest dynamics five years after ecological restoration treatments, Arizona, USA. Forest Ecology and Management. 218:129-145.

Ganey, Joseph L.; Vojta, Scott C. 2004. Characteristics of snags containing excavated cavities in northern Arizona mixed-conifer and ponderosa pine forests. Forest Ecology and Management. 199:232-332.

Grissino-Mayer, Henri D.; Romme, William H.; Floyd, M. Lisa; Hanna, David D. 2004. Climatic and human influences on fire regimes of the southern San Juan Mountains, Colorado, USA. Ecology. 85:1708-1724.

Hanks, Jess P.; Fitzhugh, E. Lee; Hanks, Sharon R. 1983. A habitat type classification system for ponderosa pine forests of northern Arizona. Gen. Tech. Rep. RM-GTR-97. Fort Collins, CO: U.S. Department of Agriculture, Forest Service, Rocky Mountain Forest and Range Experiment Station. 22 p.

Harper, Kimball T.; Ruyle, G.B.; Rittenhouse, L.R. 1988. Toxicity problems associated with the grazing of oak in intermountain and southwestern U.S.A. In: James, Lynn F.; Ralphs, Michael H.; Nielsen, Darwin B., eds. The ecology and economic impact of poisonous plants on livestock production. Boulder, CO: Westview Press: 197-206.

Harper, Kimball T.; Wagstaff, Fred J.; Kunzler, Lynn M. 1985. Biology and management of the Gambel oak vegetative type: a literature review. Gen. Tech. Rep. INT-179. Ogden, UT: U.S. Department of Agriculture, Forest Service, Intermountain Forest and Range Experiment Station. 31 p.

Harrington, M.G. 1985. The effects of spring, summer, and fall burning on Gambel oak in a southwestern ponderosa pine stand. Forest Science. 31:156-163.

Harrington, M.G. 1989. Gambel oak root carbohydrate response to spring, summer, and fall prescribed burning. Journal of Range Management. 42:504-507.

Harrington, Michael G. 1987. Phytotoxic potential of Gambel oak on ponderosa pine seed germination and initial growth. Res. Pap. RM-277. Fort Collins, CO: U.S. Department of Agriculture, Forest Service, Rocky Mountain Forest and Range Experiment Station. 7 p.

Hayward, C. Lynn. 1948. Biotic communities of the Wasatch chaparral, Utah. Ecological Monographs. 18:473-506.

Humphries, H.C.; Bourgeron, P.S. 2003. Environmental responses of *Pinus ponderosa* and associated species in the south-western USA. Journal of Biogeography. 30:257-276.

Jenness, Jeffrey S.; Beier, Paul; Ganey, Joseph L. 2004. Associations between forest fire and Mexican spotted owls. Forest Science. 50:765-772.

Klemmedson, James O. 1987. Influence of oak in pine forests of central Arizona on selected nutrients of forest floor and soil. Soil Science Society of America Journal. 51:1623-1628.

Klemmedson, James O. 1991. Oak influence on nutrient availability in pine forests of central Arizona. Soil Science Society of America Journal. 55:248-253.

18

USDA Forest Service Gen. Tech. Rep. RMRS-GTR-218. 2008

Kolb, T.E.; Stone, J.E. 2000. Differences in leaf gas exchange and water relations among species and tree sizes in an Arizona pine-oak forest. Tree Physiology. 20:1-12.

Kruse, William H. 1992. Quantifying wildlife habitats within Gambel oak/forest/woodland vegetation associations in Arizona. In: Ffolliott, Peter F.; Gottfried, Gerald J.; Bennett, Duane A.; Hernandez, C., Victor Manuel; Ortega-Rubio, Alfredo; Hamre, R.H., tech. coords. Ecology and management of oaks and associated woodlands: perspectives in the southwestern United States and northern Mexico; 1992 April 27-30; Sierra Vista, AZ. Gen. Tech. Rep. RM-218. Fort Collins, CO: U.S. Department of Agriculture, Forest Service, Rocky Mountain Forest and Range Experiment Station: 182-186.

Kunzler, L.M.; Harper, K.T. 1980. Recovery of Gambel oak after fire in central Utah. Great Basin Naturalist. 40:127-130.

Laughlin, Daniel C.; Bakker, Jonathan D.; Fulé, Peter Z. 2005. Understorey plant community structure in lower montane and subalpine forests, Grand Canyon National Park, USA. Journal of Biogeography. 32:2083-2102.

Leidolf, Andreas; Wolfe, Michael L.; Pendleton, Rosemary L. 2000. Bird communities of Gambel oak: a descriptive analysis. Gen. Tech. Rep. RMRS-GTR-48. Fort Collins, CO: U.S. Department of Agriculture, Forest Service, Rocky Mountain Research Station. 30 p.

Lesh, Tamara D. 1999. Habitat selection by selected breeding passerine birds in pine-oak forests of northern Arizona. Flagstaff, AZ: Northern Arizona University. 44 p. Thesis.

Little, Elbert L. 1971. Atlas of United States trees. Volume 1. Conifers and important hardwoods. Misc. Publ. No. 1146. U.S. Department of Agriculture, Forest Service. Washington, DC: U.S. Government Printing Office.

Long, W.H. 1941. The durability of untreated oak posts in the Southwest. Journal of Forestry. 39:701-704.

Lowell, Kim E.; Garrett, Harold E.; Mitchell, Robert J. 1989. Potential long-term growth gains from early clump thinning of coppice-regenerated oak stands. New Forests. 3:11-19.

Madany, Michael H.; West, Neil E. 1983. Livestock grazing-fire regime interactions within montane forests of Zion National Park, Utah. Ecology. 64:661-667.

Madany, Michael E.; West, Neil E. 1984. Vegetation of two relict mesas in Zion National Park. Journal of Range Management. 37:456-461.

May, Christopher A.; Gutiérrez, R.J.. 2002. Habitat associations of Mexican spotted owl nest and roost sites in central Arizona. Wilson Bulletin. 114:457-466.

May, Christopher A.; Petersburg, Mylea L.; Gutiérrez, R.J. 2004. Mexican spotted owl nest- and roost-site habitat in northern Arizona. Journal of Wildlife Management. 68:1054-1064.

McCulloch, C.Y.; Wallmo, O.C.; Ffolliott, P.F. 1965. Acorn yield of Gambel oak in northern Arizona. Res. Note RM-48. Fort Collins, CO: U.S. Department of Agriculture, Forest Service, Rocky Mountain Forest and Range Experiment Station. 2 p.

Menzel, Jody P.; Covington, W. Wallace. 1997. Changes from 1876 to 1994 in a forest ecosystem near Walnut Canyon, northern Arizona. In: van Ripler, Charles; Deshler, Elena T., eds. Proceedings of the third biennial conference of research on the Colorado Plateau; 1995; Flagstaff, AZ. Transactions and proceedings series NPS/NRNAU/NRTP-97/12, U.S. Department of the Interior, National Park Service: 151-172.

Moore, Margaret M.; Huffman, David W.; Fulé, Peter Z.; Covington, W. Wallace; Crouse, Joseph E. 2004. Comparison of historical and contemporary forest structure and composition on permanent plots in southwestern ponderosa pine forests. Forest Science. 50:162-176.

Muldavin, Esteban; Ronco, Frank; Aldon, Earl F. 1990. Consolidated stand tabls and biodiversity data base for southwestern forest habitat types. Gen. Tech. Rep. RM-190. Fort Collins, CO: U.S. Department of Agriculture, Forest Service, Rocky Mountain Forest and Range Experiment Station. 51 p.

Neff, Don J.; McCulloch, Clay Y.; Brown, David E.; Lowe, Charles H.; Barstad, Janet F. 1979. Forest, range, and watershed management for enhancement of wildlife habitat in Arizona. Special report no. 7. Phoenix, AZ: Arizona Game and Fish Department. 109 p.

Neilson, R.P.; Wullstein, L.H. 1983. Biogeography of two southwestern American oaks in relation to atmospheric dynamics. Journal of Biogeography. 10:275-297.

Neilson, Ronald P.; Wullstein, L.H. 1986. Microhabitat affinities of Gambel oak seedlings. Great Basin Naturalist. 46:294-298.

Onkonburi, Jeanmarie. 1999. Growth response of Gambel oak to thinning and burning: implications for ecological restoration. Flagstaff, AZ: Northern Arizona University. 129 p. Dissertation.

Prather, John W.; Noss, Reed F.; Sisk, Thomas D. 2008. Real versus perceived conflicts between restoration of ponderosa pine forests and conservation of the Mexican spotted owl. Forest Policy and Economics. 10:140-150.

Reynolds, Hudson G.; Clary, Warren P.; Ffolliott, Peter F. 1970. Gambel oak for southwestern wildlife. Journal of Forestry. 68:545-547.

Roccaforte, John Paul. 2005. Monitoring landscape-scale forest structure and potential fire behavior changes following ponderosa pine restoration treatments. Flagstaff, AZ: Northern Arizona University. 102 p. Thesis.

Rosenstock, Steven S. 1998. Influence of Gambel oak on breeding birds in ponderosa pine forests of northern Arizona. Condor. 100:485-492.

Rowe, J.S. 1983. Concepts of fire effects on plant individuals and species. In: Wein, Ross W.; MacLean, David A., eds. The role of fire in northern circumpolar ecosystems. New York, NY: John Wiley and Sons: 135-154.

Ruess, Bradley J. 1995. Changes in Mexican spotted owl habitat within ponderosa pine/Gambel oak communities since Euro-American settlement. Flagstaff, AZ: Northern Arizona University. 42 p. Thesis.

Ryniker, K.A.; Bush, J.K.; Van Auken, O.W. 2006. Structure of *Quercus gambelii* communities in the Lincoln National Forest, New Mexico, USA. Forest Ecology and Management. 233:69-77.

Savage, Melissa; Mast, Joy Nystrom. 2005. How resilient are southwestern ponderosa pine forests after crown fires? Canadian Journal of Forest Research. 35:967-977.

Seamans, Mark E.; Gutiérrez, R.J.; May, Christopher A.; Perry, M. Zachariah. 1999. Demography of two Mexican spotted owl populations. Conservation Biology. 13:744-754.

Society for Ecological Restoration International Science and Policy Working Group. 2004. The SER international primer on ecological restoration. Tucson, AZ: Society for Ecological Restoration International. 13 p.

Shipek, D. Catlow; Ffolliott, Peter F.; Gottfried, Gerald J.; DeBano, Leonard F. 2004. Transpiration and multiple use management of thinned Emory oak coppice. Res. Pap. RMRS-RP-48. Fort Collins, CO: U.S. Department of Agriculture, Forest Service, Rocky Mountain Research Station. 8 p.

Simonin, Kevin A. 2000. *Quercus gambelii*. In: Fire effects information system [online]. U.S. Department of Agriculture, Forest Service, Rocky Mountain Research Station, Fire Sciences Laboratory. Available: http://www.fs.fed.us/database/feis/ [2005, June 20].

Sopp, D.F; Salac, S.S.; Sutton, R.K. 1977. Germination of Gambel oak seed. Tree Planter's Notes. 28:4-5.

Swetnam, Thomas W.; Brown, Peter M. 1992. Oldest known conifers in the southwestern United States: temporal and spatial patterns of maximum age. In: Kaufmann, Merrill R.; Moir, W.H.; Bassett, Richard L., tech. coords. Old-growth forests in the Southwest and Rocky Mountain Regions: proceedings of a workshop; 1992 March 9-13; Portal, AZ. Gen. Tech. Rep. RM-213. Fort Collins, CO: U.S. Department of Agriculture, Rocky Mountain Forest and Range Experiment Station: 24-38.

USDA Forest Service Gen. Tech. Rep. RMRS-GTR-218. 2008

19

Swetnam, Thomas W.; Dieterich, John H. 1985. Fire history of ponderosa pine forests in the Gila Wilderness, New Mexico. In: Lotan, James E.; Kilgore, B.M.; Fischer, W.C.; Mutch R.W., tech. coords. Proceedings—symposium and workshop on wilderness fire: 1983 November 15-18; Missoula, MT. Gen. Tech. Rep. INT-182. Ogden UT: U.S. Department of Agriculture, Forest Service, Intermountain Forest and Range Experiment Station: 390-397.

Tew, Ronald K. 1967. Soil moisture depletion by Gambel oak in central Utah. Res. Note INT-74. Ogden, UT: U.S. Department of Agriculture, Forest Service, Intermountain Forest and Range Experiment Station. 8 p.

Tiedemann, A.R.; Clary, W.P.; Barbour, R.J. 1987. Underground systems of Gambel oak (*Quercus gambelii*) in central Utah. American Journal of Botany. 74:1065-1071.

Touchan, Ramzi; Ffolliott, Peter F. 1999. Thinning of Emory oak coppice: effects on growth, yield, and harvesting cycles. Southwestern Naturalist. 44:1-5.

Van Auken, O.W. 2000. Shrub invasions of North American semiarid grasslands. Annual Review of Ecology and Systematics. 31:197-215.

Wagstaff, Fred J. 1984. Economic considerations in use and management of Gambel oak for fuelwood. Gen. Tech. Rep. INT-165. Ogden, UT: U.S. Department of Agriculture, Forest Service, Intermountain Forest and Range Experiment Station. 8 p.

Wallin, Kimberly F.; Kolb, Thomas E.; Skov, Kjerstin R.; Wagner, Michael R. 2004. Seven-year results of thinning and burning restoration treatments on old ponderosa pines at the Gus Pearson Natural Area. Restoration Ecology. 12:239-247.

Waltz, Amy E.M.; Fulé, Peter Z.; Covington, W. Wallace; Moore, Margaret M. 2003. Diversity in ponderosa pine forest structure following ecological restoration treatments. Forest Science. 49:885-900.

Wightman, Catherine S.; Germaine, Stephen S. 2006. Forest stand characteristics altered by restoration affect western bluebird habitat quality. Restoration Ecology. 14:653-661.

Younberg, C.T. 1975. Effects of fertilization and thinning on the growth of ponderosa pine. Soil Science Society of America Proceedings. 39:137-139.

20

USDA Forest Service Gen. Tech. Rep. RMRS-GTR-218. 2008

Appendix _____

Categorized Gambel oak references, including oak references cited in this report and additional references, placed into 11 categories. Reference lists were obtained by searching:

1. scientific databases (Agricola, Biological Sciences, and Google Scholar [http://scholar.google.com/])
2. Forest Service databases (Fire Effects Information System [http://www.fs.fed.us/database/feis/] and Rocky Mountain Research Station publications)
3. reference lists in located articles

The search words were Gambel oak and *Quercus gambelii*. Category 7 (wildlife and invertebrate habitat) is intended only to provide examples of the diverse literature on Gambel oak-wildlife relationships. Similarly, the list is not intended to be exhaustive on all subjects (for example, oak genetics). Some references in the list could be classified into multiple categories, and these references were classified into the one category each most closely matched.

1. Synthesis Articles

Clary, Warren P.; Tiedemann, Arthur R. 1992. Ecology and values of Gambel oak woodlands. In: Ffolliott, Peter F.; Gottfried, Gerald J.; Bennett, Duane A.; Hernandez, C., Victor Manuel; Ortega-Rubio, Alfredo; Hamre, R.H., tech. coords. Ecology and management of oaks and associated woodlands: perspectives in the southwestern United States and northern Mexico; 1992 April 27-30; Sierra Vista, AZ. Gen. Tech. Rep. RM-218. Fort Collins, CO: U.S. Department of Agriculture, Forest Service, Rocky Mountain Forest and Range Experiment Station: 87-95.

Harper, Kimball T.; Wagstaff, Fred J.; Kunzler, Lynn M. 1985. Biology and management of the Gambel oak vegetative type: a literature review. Gen. Tech. Rep. INT-179. Ogden, UT: U.S. Department of Agriculture, Forest Service, Intermountain Forest and Range Experiment Station. 31 p.

Horton, L.E. 1975. An abstract bibliography of Gambel oak (*Quercus gambelii* Nutt.). Ogden, UT: U.S. Department of Agriculture, Forest Service, Intermountain Region. 64 p.

Leidolf, Andreas; Wolfe, Michael L.; Pendleton, Rosemary L. 2000. Bird communities of Gambel oak: a descriptive analysis. Gen. Tech. Rep. RMRS-GTR-48. Fort Collins, CO: U.S. Department of Agriculture, Forest Service, Rocky Mountain Research Station. 30 p.

2. Biological and Ecological Characteristics

Abella, Scott R. 2008. Gambel oak growth forms: management opportunities for increasing ecosystem diversity. Res. Note RMRS-RN-37. Fort Collins, CO: U.S. Department of Agriculture, Forest Service, Rocky Mountain Research Station. 6 p.

Allman, Verl Phillips. 1953. A preliminary study of the vegetation in an exclosure in the chaparral of the Wasatch Mountains, Utah. Utah Academy of Sciences, Arts and Letters Proceedings. 30:63-78.

Antonijevic, Zoran. 1992. Gambel oak reproduction in southwestern ponderosa pine forests. Flagstaff, AZ: Northern Arizona University. 48 p. Thesis.

Baker, F.S.; Korstian, Clarence F. 1931. Suitability of the brush lands in the Intermountain region for the growth of natural or planted western yellow pine forests. Tech. Bull. 256. Washington, DC: U.S. Department of Agriculture. 82 p.

Barger, Roland L.; Ffolliott, Peter F. 1964. Specific gravity of Arizona Gambel oak. Res. Note RM-19. Fort Collins, CO: U.S. Department of Agriculture, Forest Service, Rocky Mountain Forest and Range Experiment Station. 2 p.

Brady, Ward; Bonham, Charles D. 1976. Vegetation patterns on an altitudinal gradient, Huachuca Mountains, Arizona. Southwestern Naturalist. 21:55-66.

Baker, William L. 1949. Soil changes associated with recovery of scrub oak, *Quercus gambelii*, after fire. Salt Lake City, UT: University of Utah. 65 p. Thesis.

Brischler, Erik J. 2002. Size structure and spatial arrangement of Gambel oak in northern Arizona. Flagstaff, AZ: Northern Arizona University. 128 p. Thesis.

Brotherson, J.D.; Rushforth, S.R.; Evenson, W.E.; Johansen, J.R.; Morden, C. 1983. Population dynamics and age relationships of eight tree species in Navajo National Monument, Arizona. Journal of Range Management. 36:250-256.

Brown, Roy C.; Mogensen, H. Lloyd. 1972. Late ovule and early embryo development in *Quercus gambelii*. American Journal of Botany. 59:311-316.

Christensen, Earl M. 1950. Distributional observations of oak brush (*Quercus gambelii* Nutt.) in Utah. Utah Academy of Sciences, Arts and Letters Proceedings. 27:22-25.

Christensen, Earl M. 1955. Ecological notes on the mountain brush in Utah. Utah Academy of Sciences, Arts and Letters Proceedings. 32:107-111.

Cottam, Walter P.; Tucker, John M.; Drobnick, Rudy. 1959. Some clues to Great Basin postpluvial climates provided by oak distributions. Ecology. 49:361-377.

González, Grizelle; Seastedt, Timothy R. 2001. Soil fauna and plant litter decomposition in tropical and subalpine forests. Ecology. 82:955-964.

Grover, B.L.; Richardson, E.A.; Southard, A.R. 1970. *Quercus gambelii* as an indicator of climatic means. Utah Academy of Science Proceedings. 47(part 1):187-191.

Hanks, Jess P.; Fitzhugh, E. Lee; Hanks, Sharon R. 1983. A habitat type classification system for ponderosa pine forests of northern Arizona. Gen. Tech. Rep. RM-GTR-97. Fort Collins, CO: U.S. Department of Agriculture, Forest Service, Rocky Mountain Forest and Range Experiment Station. 22 p.

Harley, Peter; Deem, Greg; Flint, Stephan; Caldwell, Martyn. 1996. Effects of growth under elevated UV-B on photosynthesis and isoprene emission in *Quercus gambelii* and *Mucuna pruriens*. Global Change Biology. 2:149-154.

Humphries, H.C.; Bourgeron, P.S. 2003. Environmental responses of *Pinus ponderosa* and associated species in the south-western USA. Journal of Biogeography. 30:257-276.

Kumar, A.; Rogstad, S.H. 1998. A hierarchical analysis of minisatellite DNA diversity in Gambel oak (*Quercus gambelii* Nutt.; Fagaceae). Molecular Ecology. 7:859-869.

Kunzler, L.M.; Harper, K.T.; Kunzler, D.B. 1981. Compositional similarity within the oakbrush type in central and northern Utah. Great Basin Naturalist. 41:147-153.

Laughlin, Daniel C.; Bakker, Jonathan D.; Fulé, Peter Z. 2005. Understorey plant community structure in lower montane and subalpine forests, Grand Canyon National Park, USA. Journal of Biogeography. 32:2083-2102.

Loehle, Craig. 1988. Tree life history strategies: the role of defenses. Canadian Journal of Forest Research. 18:209-222.

Long, W.H. 1941. The durability of untreated oak posts in the Southwest. Journal of Forestry. 39:701-704.

Maze, Jack. 1968. Past hybridization between *Quercus macrocarpa* and *Quercus gambelii*. Brittonia. 20:321-333.

USDA Forest Service Gen. Tech. Rep. RMRS-GTR-218. 2008

21

McCulloch, C.Y.; Wallmo, O.C.; Ffolliott, P.F. 1965. Acorn yield of Gambel oak in northern Arizona. Res. Note RM-48. Fort Collins, CO: U.S. Department of Agriculture, Forest Service, Rocky Mountain Forest and Range Experiment Station. 2 p.

Mogensen, H. Lloyd. 1973. Some histochemical, ultrastructural, and nutritional aspects of the ovule of *Quercus gambelii*. American Journal of Botany. 60:48-54.

Muldavin, Esteban; Ronco, Frank; Aldon, Earl F. 1990. Consolidated stand tables and biodiversity data base for southwestern forest habitat types. Gen. Tech. Rep. RM-190. Fort Collins, CO: U.S. Department of Agriculture, Forest Service, Rocky Mountain Forest and Range Experiment Station. 51 p.

Neilson, R.P.; Wullstein, L.H. 1983. Biogeography of two southwestern American oaks in relation to atmospheric dynamics. Journal of Biogeography. 10:275-297.

Neilson, R.P.; Wullstein, L.H. 1980. Catkin freezing and acorn production in Gambel oak in Utah, 1978. American Journal of Botany. 67:426-428.

Neilson, Ronald P.; Wullstein, L.H. 1986. Microhabitat affinities of Gambel oak seedlings. Great Basin Naturalist. 46:294-298.

Nemati, Nasser; Goetz, Harold. 1995. Relationships of overstory to understory cover variables in a ponderosa pine/Gambel oak ecosystem. Vegetatio. 119:15-21.

Nixon, Elray S. 1967. A comparative study of the mountain brush vegetation in Utah. Great Basin Naturalist. 27:59-66.

Norton, J.B.; Sandor, J.A.; White, C.S. 2003. Hillslope soils and organic matter dynamics within a Native American agroecosystem on the Colorado Plateau. Soil Science Society of America Journal. 67:225-234.

Pendleton, Rosemary L.; Sanderson, Stewart C.; McArthur, E. Durant. 1985. Morphologic and enzymatic variability among Gambel oak clones in northcentral Utah. In: Johnson, Kendall L., ed. Proceedings of the Third Utah Shrub Ecology Workshop; 1983 August 30-31; Provo, UT. Logan, UT: Utah State University: 19-28.

Reynolds, Jamie L.; Feinstein, Timothy N.; Ebersole, James J. 2000. Sexual reproduction of Gambel oak (*Quercus gambelii*) near its northeastern limit. Western North American Naturalist. 60:225-227.

Ryniker, K.A.; Bush, J.K.; Van Auken, O.W. 2006. Structure of *Quercus gambelii* communities in the Lincoln National Forest, New Mexico, USA. Forest Ecology and Management. 233:69-77.

Sackett, Stephen S. 1980. Woody fuel particle size and specific gravity of southwestern tree species. Res. Note RM-389. Fort Collins, CO: U.S. Department of Agriculture, Forest Service, Rocky Mountain Forest and Range Experiment Station. 4 p.

Sampson, Arthur W.; Samisch, Rudolf. 1935. Growth and seasonal changes in composition of oak leaves. Plant Physiology. 10:739-751.

Schier, George A. 1983. Vegetative regeneration of Gambel oak and chokecherry from excised rhizomes. Forest Science. 29:499-502.

Schnabel, Andrew; Hamrick, J.L. 1990. Comparative analysis of population genetic structure in *Quercus macrocarpa* and *Q. gambelii* (Fagaceae). Systematic Botany. 15:240-251.

Sopp, D.F; Salac, S.S.; Sutton, R.K. 1977. Germination of Gambel oak seed. Tree Planter's Notes. 28:4-5.

Swetnam, Thomas W.; Brown, Peter M. 1992. Oldest known conifers in the southwestern United States: temporal and spatial patterns of maximum age. In: Kaufmann, Merrill R.; Moir, W.H.; Bassett, Richard L., tech. coords. Old-growth forests in the Southwest and Rocky Mountain Regions: proceedings of a workshop; 1992 March 9-13; Portal, AZ. Gen. Tech. Rep. RM-213. Fort Collins, CO: U.S. Department of Agriculture, Rocky Mountain Forest and Range Experiment Station: 24-38.

Tiedemann, A.R.; Clary, W.P.; Barbour, R.J. 1987. Underground systems of Gambel oak (*Quercus gambelii*) in central Utah. American Journal of Botany. 74:1065-1071.

Tucker, J.M.; Neilson, R.P.; Wullstein, L.H. 1980. Hermaphroditic flowering in Gambel oak. American Journal of Botany. 67:1265-1267.

Williams, Joseph H.; Boecklen, William J.; Howard, Daniel J. 2001. Reproductive processes in two oak (*Quercus*) contact zones with different levels of hybridization. Heredity. 87:680-690.

Wright, H.E.; Bent, Anne M.; Hansen, Barbara Spross; Maher, L.J. 1973. Present and past vegetation of the Chuska Mountains, northwestern New Mexico. Geological Society of America Bulletin. 51:1155-1180.

Wullstein, L.H.; Neilson, R.P. 1985. Seedling survival and biogeography of Gambel oak (*Quercus gambelii*) in northern Utah. In: Johnson, Kendall L., ed. Proceedings of the Third Utah Shrub Ecology Workshop; 1983 August 30-31; Provo, UT. Logan, UT: Utah State University: 1-3.

3. Growth and Wood Production

Adams, Henry D.; Kolb, Thomas E. 2005. Tree growth response to drought and temperature in a mountain landscape in northern Arizona, USA. Journal of Biogeography. 32:1629-1640.

Barger, Roland L.; Ffolliott, Peter F. 1972. Physical characteristics and utilization of major woodland tree species in Arizona. Res. Pap. RM-83. Fort Collins, CO: U.S. Department of Agriculture, Forest Service, Rocky Mountain Forest and Range Experiment Station. 80 p.

Bechtold, William A. 2004. Largest-crown-width prediction models for 53 species in the western United States. Western Journal of Applied Forestry. 19:245-251.

Chojnacky, David C. 1988. Juniper, pinyon, oak, and mesquite volume equations for Arizona. Res. Pap. INT-391. Ogden, UT: U.S. Department of Agriculture, Forest Service, Intermountain Research Station. 11 p.

Chojnacky, David C.; Rogers, Paul. 1999. Converting tree diameter measured at root collar to diameter at breast height. Western Journal of Applied Forestry. 14:14-16.

Clary, Warren P.; Ffolliott, Peter F.; Larson, Frederic R. 1984. Producer-consumer biomass in montane forests on the Arizona Mogollon Plateau. Great Basin Naturalist. 44:627-634.

Clary, Warren P.; Tiedemann, Arthur R. 1985. Biomass distribution in northcentral Utah Gambel oak stands. In: Johnson, Kendall L., ed. Proceedings of the Third Utah Shrub Ecology Workshop; 1983 August 30-31; Provo, UT. Logan, UT: Utah State University: 9-12.

Clary, Warren P.; Tiedemann, Arthur R. 1986. Distribution of biomass within small tree and shrub form *Quercus gambelii* stands. Forest Science. 32:234-242.

Clary, Warren P.; Tiedemann, Arthur R. 1987. Fuelwood potential in large-tree *Quercus gambelii* stands. Western Journal of Applied Forestry. 2:87-90.

Clary, Warren P.; Tiedemann, Arthur R. 1993. Bole volume growth in stems of *Quercus gambelii*. Great Basin Naturalist. 53:162-167.

Johnson, K.L. 1985. Volume and biomass on Gambel oak woodlands. In: Van Hooser, Dwane D.; Van Pelt, Nicholas, comps. Proceedings – growth and yield and other mensurational tricks: a regional technical conference; 1984 November 6-7; Logan, UT. Gen. Tech. Rep. INT-193. Ogden, UT: U.S. Department of Agriculture, Forest Service, Intermountain Forest and Range Experiment Station: 82-85.

Van Hooser, Dwane D.; Schaefer, James C. 1985. Status of forest survey of Gambel oak in the Four Corner States. In: Johnson, Kendall L., ed. Proceedings of the Third Utah Shrub Ecology Workshop; 1983 August 30-31; Provo, UT. Logan, UT: Utah State University: 5-8.

Wagstaff, Fred J. 1984. Economic considerations in use and management of Gambel oak for fuelwood. Gen. Tech. Rep. INT-165. Ogden, UT: U.S. Department of Agriculture, Forest Service, Intermountain Forest and Range Experiment Station. 8 p.

Wagstaff, Fred J. 1985. Economics of using Gambel oak for firewood. In: Johnson, Kendall L., ed. Proceedings of the Third Utah Shrub Ecology Workshop; 1983 August 30-31; Provo, UT. Logan, UT: Utah State University: 53-58.

4. Effects on Soils

Klemmedson, James O. 1987. Influence of oak in pine forests of central Arizona on selected nutrients of forest floor and soil. Soil Science Society of America Journal. 51:1623-1628.

Klemmedson, James O. 1991. Oak influence on nutrient availability in pine forests of central Arizona. Soil Science Society of America Journal. 55:248-253.

Klemmedson, James O. 1992. Decomposition and nutrient release from mixtures of Gambel oak and ponderosa pine leaf litter. Forest Ecology and Management. 47:349-361.

Lefevre, R.E.; Klemmedson, J.O. 1980. Effect of Gambel oak on forest floor and soil of a ponderosa pine forest. Soil Science Society of America Journal. 44:842-846.

Shukla, M.K.; Lal, R.; Ebinger, M.; Meyer, C. 2006. Physical and chemical properties of soils under some piñon-juniper-oak canopies in a semi-arid ecosystem in New Mexico. Journal of Arid Environments. 66:673-685.

Tiedemann, A.R.; Clary, W.P. 1996. Nutrient distribution in *Quercus gambelii* stands in central Utah. Great Basin Naturalist. 56:119-128.

Tiedemann, Arthur R.; Clary, Warren P. 1985. Nitrogen distribution in northcentral Utah Gambel oak stands. In: Johnson, Kendall L., ed. Proceedings of the Third Utah Shrub Ecology Workshop; 1983 August 30-31; Provo, UT. Logan, UT: Utah State University: 13-18.

5. Effects on Understory Vegetation

Abella, Scott R. In prep. Tree canopy types constrain plant distributions in ponderosa pine-Gambel oak forests, northern Arizona. Res. Note RMRS-RN-##. Fort Collins, CO: U.S. Department of Agriculture, Forest Service, Rocky Mountain Research Station.

Abella, Scott R.; Springer, Judith D. 2008. Canopy-tree influences along a soil parent material gradient in *Pinus-ponderosa-Quercus gambelii* forests, northern Arizona. Journal of the Torrey Botanical Society. 135:26-36.

Brown, Harry E. 1958. Gambel oak in west-central Colorado. Ecology. 39:317-327.

Evenson, William E.; Brotherson, Jack D.; Wilcox, Richard B. 1980. Relationship between environmental and vegetational parameters for understory and open-area communities. Great Basin Naturalist. 40:167-174.

Haile, A. 1984. A study of the effects of oak defoliation on understory plants. Journal of Agricultural Science. 102:247-249.

Madany, Michael E.; West, Neil E. 1984. Vegetation of two relict mesas in Zion National Park. Journal of Range Management. 37:456-461.

Moinat, A.D. 1956. Comparative yields of herbage from oak scrub and interspersed grassland in Colorado. Ecology. 37:852-854.

Wilcox, Richard B.; Brotherson, Jack D.; Evenson, William E. 1981. Canopy influence on understory community composition. Northwest Science. 55:194-201.

6. Water Use and Competition With Pine

Abella, Scott R.; Fulé, Peter Z.; Covington, W. Wallace. 2006. Diameter caps for thinning southwestern ponderosa pine forests: viewpoints, effects, and tradeoffs. Journal of Forestry. 104:407-414.

Biondi, Franco; Klemmedson, James O.; Kuehl, Robert O. 1992. Dendrochronological analysis of single-tree interactions in mixed pine-oak stands of central Arizona, USA. Forest Ecology and Management. 48:321-333.

Dina, Stephen J.; Klikoff, Lionel G. 1973. Carbon dioxide exchange by several streamside and scrub oak community species of Red Butte Canyon, Utah. American Midland Naturalist. 89:70-80.

Dina, Stephen J.; Klikoff, Lionel G.; Keddington, Michael B. 1973. Seasonal water potential patterns in the mountain brush zone, Utah. American Midland Naturalist. 89:234-239.

Harrington, Michael G. 1987. Phytotoxic potential of Gambel oak on ponderosa pine seed germination and initial growth. Res. Pap. RM-277. Fort Collins, CO: U.S. Department of Agriculture, Forest Service, Rocky Mountain Forest and Range Experiment Station. 7 p.

Kolb, T.E.; Stone, J.E. 2000. Differences in leaf gas exchange and water relations among species and tree sizes in an Arizona pine-oak forest. Tree Physiology. 20:1-12.

Neilson, Ronald P.; Wullstein, L.H. 1985. Comparative drought physiology and biogeography of *Quercus gambelii* and *Quercus turbinella*. American Midland Naturalist. 114:259-271.

Phillips, Susan L.; Ehleringer, James R. 1995. Limited uptake of summer precipitation by bigtooth maple (*Acer grandidentatum* Nutt) and Gambel's oak (*Quercus gambelii* Nutt). Trees: Structure and Function. 9:214-219.

Tew, Ronald K. 1966. Soil moisture depletion by Gambel oak in northern Utah. Res. Note INT-54. Ogden, UT: U.S. Department of Agriculture, Forest Service, Intermountain Forest and Range Experiment Station. 7 p.

Tew, Ronald K. 1967. Soil moisture depletion by Gambel oak in central Utah. Res. Note INT-74. Ogden, UT: U.S. Department of Agriculture, Forest Service, Intermountain Forest and Range Experiment Station. 8 p.

Tew, Ronald K. 1969. Converting Gambel oak sites to grass reduces soil-moisture depletion. Res. Note INT-104. Ogden, UT: U.S. Department of Agriculture, Forest Service, Intermountain Forest and Range Experiment Station. 4 p.

Williams, David G.; Ehleringer, James R. 1996. Carbon isotope discrimination in three semi-arid woodland species along a monsoon gradient. Oecologia. 106:455-460.

Williams, David G.; Ehleringer, James R. 2000. Carbon isotope discrimination and water relations in oak hybrid populations in southwestern Utah. Western North American Naturalist. 60:121-129.

Williams, David G.; Ehleringer, James R. 2000. Intra-and inter-specific variation for summer precipitation use in pinyon-juniper woodlands. Ecological Monographs. 70:517-537.

7. Wildlife and Invertebrate Habitat

Aguilar, Jeffrey M.; Boecklen, William J. 1992. Patterns of herbivory in the *Quercus grisea × Quercus gambelii* species complex. Oikos. 64:498-504.

Arsenault, D.P. 2004. Differentiating nest sites of primary and secondary cavity-nesting birds in New Mexico. Journal of Field Ornithology. 75:257-265.

Bernardos, D.A. 2001. Use of ponderosa pine-Gambel oak forests by bats in northern Arizona. Flagstaff, AZ: Northern Arizona University. Thesis. 79 p.

Bernardos, Debra A.; Chambers, Carol L.; Rabe, Michael J. 2004. Selection of Gambel oak roosts by southwestern myotis in ponderosa pine-dominated forests, northern Arizona. Journal of Wildlife Management. 68:595-601.

Brawn, Jeffrey D.; Balda, Russell P. 1988. Population biology of cavity nesters in northern Arizona: do nest sites limit breeding densities? Condor. 90:61-71.

Brotherson, J.D.; Szyska, L.A.; Evenson, W.E. 1981. Bird community composition in relation to habitat and season in Betatakin Canyon, Navajo National Monument, Arizona. Great Basin Naturalist. 41:298-309.

Campbell, Steven P.; Boecklen, William J. 2002. Are plant hybrid zones centers of vertebrate biodiversity? A test in the *Quercus grisea × Quercus gambelii* species complex. Biodiversity and Conservation. 11:443-467.

USDA Forest Service Gen. Tech. Rep. RMRS-GTR-218. 2008

23

Chambers, Carol L. 2002. Forest management and the dead wood resource in ponderosa pine forests: effects on small mammals. In: Laudenslayer, William F.; Shea, Patrick J.; Valentine, Bradley E.; Weatherspoon, Phillip; Lisle, Thomas E., tech. coords. Proceedings of the symposium on the ecology and management of dead wood in western forests; 1999 November 2-4; Reno, NV. Gen. Tech. Rep. PSW-GTR-181. Albany, CA: U.S. Department of Agriculture, Forest Service, Pacific Southwest Research Station: 679-693.

Cunningham, J.B.; Balda, R.P.; Gaud, W.S. 1980. Selection and use of snags by cavity-nesting birds of the ponderosa pine forest. Res. Pap. RM-222. U.S. Department of Agriculture, Forest Service, Rocky Mountain Forest and Range Experiment Station, Fort Collins, CO. 15 p.

Faeth, Stanley H.; Rooney, Robert F. 1993. Variable budbreak and insect folivory of Gambel oak (*Quercus gambelii* Fagaceae). Southwestern Naturalist. 38:1-8.

Fischer, Jan Mary. 1978. A natural history study of the Virginia's warbler (*Vermivora virginiae*) in the ponderosa pine community. Flagstaff, AZ: Northern Arizona University. 87 p. Thesis.

Fleck, David C.; Tomback, Diana F. 1996. Tannin and protein in the diet of a food-hoarding granivore, the western scrub-jay. Condor. 98:474-482.

Ganey, Joseph L. 1999. Snag density and composition of snag populations on two national forests in northern Arizona. Forest Ecology and Management. 117:169-178.

Ganey, J.L., W.M. Block, J.S. Jenness, and R.A. Wilson. 1999. Mexican spotted owl home range and habitat use in pine-oak forest: implications for forest management. Forest Science. 45:127-135.

Ganey, Joseph L.; Benoit, Mary Ann. 2002. Using terrestrial ecosystem survey data to identify potential habitat for the Mexican spotted owl on national forest system lands: a pilot study. Gen. Tech. Rep. RMRS-GTR-86. Fort Collins, CO: U.S. Department of Agriculture, Forest Service, Rocky Mountain Research Station, 25 p.

Ganey, Joseph L.; Vojta, Scott C. 2004. Characteristics of snags containing excavated cavities in northern Arizona mixed-conifer and ponderosa pine forests. Forest Ecology and Management. 199:232-332.

Gaylord, Eric S.; Preszler, Ralph W.; Boecklen, William J. 1996. Interactions between host plants, endophytic fungi, and a phytophagous insect in an oak (*Quercus grisea* × *Q. gambelii*) hybrid zone. Oecologia. 105:336-342.

Hayward, C. Lynn. 1948. Biotic communities of the Wasatch chaparral, Utah. Ecological Monographs. 18:473-506.

Jentsch, S.A. 2005. Associations among breeding birds and characteristics of Gambel oak in ponderosa pine forests. Tucson, AZ: University of Arizona. 59 p. Thesis.

Kruse, William H. 1992. Quantifying wildlife habitats within Gambel oak/forest/woodland vegetation associations in Arizona. In: Ffolliott, Peter F.; Gottfried, Gerald J.; Bennett, Duane A.; Hernandez, C., Victor Manuel; Ortega-Rubio, Alfredo; Hamre, R.H., tech. coords. Ecology and management of oaks and associated woodlands: perspectives in the southwestern United States and northern Mexico; 1992 April 27-30; Sierra Vista, AZ. Gen. Tech. Rep. RM-218. Fort Collins, CO: U.S. Department of Agriculture, Forest Service, Rocky Mountain Forest and Range Experiment Station: 182-186.

Larson, Frederic R.; Ffolliott, Peter F.; Clary, Warren P. 1986. Managing wildlife habitat: in southwestern ponderosa pine forests, diverse treatments are the key. Journal of Forestry. 84:40-41.

Lesh, Tamara D. 1999. Habitat selection by selected breeding passerine birds in pine-oak forests of northern Arizona. Flagstaff, AZ: Northern Arizona University. 44 p. Thesis.

Lightfoot, David C. 1996. A comparison of ground-dwelling arthropod assemblages among different habitats resulting from the 1977 La Mesa Fire. In: Allen, Craig D., tech. ed. Fire effects in southwestern forests: proceedings of the second La Mesa Fire symposium; 1994 March 29-31; Los Alamos, NM. Gen. Tech. Rep. RM-GTR-286. Fort Collins, CO: U.S. Department of Agriculture, Forest Service, Rocky Mountain Forest and Range Experiment Station: 166-178.

Lindsey, J. Page. 1985. Basidiomycetes that decay Gambel oak in southwestern Colorado. Mycotaxon. 22:327-362.

Lindsey, J. Page. 1986. Basidiomycetes that decay Gambel oak in southwestern Colorado: II. Mycotaxon. 25:67-83.

Lindsey, J. Page. 1986. Basidiomycetes that decay Gambel oak in southwestern Colorado. III. Mycotaxon. 27:325-345.

Marti, C.D. 1977. Avian use of an oakbrush community in northern Utah. Southwestern Naturalist. 22:367-374.

May, Christopher A.; Gutiérrez, R.J. 2002. Habitat associations of Mexican spotted owl nest and roost sites in central Arizona. Wilson Bulletin. 114:457-466.

May, Christopher A.; Petersburg, Mylea L.; Gutiérrez, R.J. 2004. Mexican spotted owl nest- and roost-site habitat in northern Arizona. Journal of Wildlife Management. 68:1054-1064.

Neff, Don J.; McCulloch, Clay Y.; Brown, David E.; Lowe, Charles H.; Barstad, Janet F. 1979. Forest, range, and watershed management for enhancement of wildlife habitat in Arizona. Special report no. 7. Phoenix, AZ: Arizona Game and Fish Department. 109 p.

Ortega, C.P.; Ortega, J.C. 2003. Comparison of black-headed grosbeaks nesting in riparian and Gambel oak pastures in southwestern Colorado. Southwestern Naturalist 48:383-388.

Passovoy, M. David; Fulé, Peter Z. 2006. Snag and woody debris dynamics following severe wildfires in northern Arizona ponderosa pine forests. Forest Ecology and Management. 223:237-246.

Patton, D.R.; Green, W. 1970. Abert's squirrel prefer mature ponderosa pine. Res. Note RM-169. Fort Collins, CO: U.S. Department of Agriculture, Forest Service, Rocky Mountain Forest and Range Experiment Station. 3 p.

Patton, David R. 1975. Abert squirrel cover requirements in southwestern ponderosa pine. Res. Pap. RM-145. Fort Collins, CO: U.S. Department of Agriculture, Forest Service, Rocky Mountain Forest and Range Experiment Station. 12 p.

Reynolds, Hudson G.; Clary, Warren P.; Ffolliott, Peter F. 1970. Gambel oak for southwestern wildlife. Journal of Forestry. 68:545-547.

Rosenstock, Steven S. 1998. Influence of Gambel oak on breeding birds in ponderosa pine forests of northern Arizona. Condor. 100:485-492.

Seamans, Mark E.; Gutiérrez, R.J.; May, Christopher A.; Perry, M. Zachariah. 1999. Demography of two Mexican spotted owl populations. Conservation Biology. 13:744-754.

Steinhoff, Harold W. 1978. Management of Gambel oak associations for wildlife and livestock. Unpublished paper on file at: U.S. Department of Agriculture, Forest Service, Rocky Mountain Research Station, Fort Collins, CO. 119 p.

Ward, James P.; Block, William M. 1995. Chapter 5: Mexican spotted owl prey ecology. In Mexican spotted owl recover plan, volume II. U.S. Department of the Interior, Fish and Wildlife Service.

Wightman, Catherine S.; Germaine, Stephen S. 2006. Forest stand characteristics altered by restoration affect western bluebird habitat quality. Restoration Ecology. 14:653-661.

Yarnes, Christopher T.; Boecklen, William J. 2005. Abiotic factors promote plant heterogeneity and influence herbivore performance and mortality in Gambel's oak (*Quercus gambelii*). Entomologia Experimentalis et Applicata. 114:87-95.

Yarnes, Christopher T.; Boecklen, William J. 2006. Abiotic mosaics affect seasonal variation of plant resources and influence the performance and mortality of a leaf-miner in Gambel's oak (*Quercus gambelii*, Nutt.). Ecological Research. 21:157-163.

24

USDA Forest Service Gen. Tech. Rep. RMRS-GTR-218. 2008

8. Browse Production

Dick, Brian L.; Urness, Philip J. 1991. Nutritional value of fresh Gambel oak browse for Spanish goats. Journal of Range Management. 44:361-364.

Harper, Kimball T.; Ruyle, G.B.; Rittenhouse, L.R. 1988. Toxicity problems associated with the grazing of oak in intermountain and southwestern U.S.A. In: James, Lynn F.; Ralphs, Michael H.; Nielsen, Darwin B., eds. The ecology and economic impact of poisonous plants on livestock production. Boulder, CO: Westview Press: 197-206.

Hutchings, Selar S.; Mason, Lamar R. 1970. Estimating yields of Gambel oak from foliage cover and basal area. Journal of Range Management. 23:430-434.

Jefferies, N.W. 1965. Herbage production on a Gambel oak range in southwestern Colorado. Journal of Range Management. 18:212-213.

Kufeld, Roland C.; Stevens, Marilyn; Bowden, David C. 1981. Winter variation in nutrient and fiber content and in vitro digestibility of Gambel oak (*Quercus gambelii*) and big sagebrush (*Artemisia tridentata*) from diversified sites in Colorado. Journal of Range Management. 34:149-151.

Nastis, A.S.; Malechek, J.C. 1981. Digestion and utilization of nutrients in oak browse by goats. Journal of Animal Science. 53:283-290.

Nastis, Anastasios S.; Malechek, John C. 1988. Estimating digestibility of oak Browne diets for goats by in vitro techniques. Journal of Range Management. 41:255-258.

Pendleton, Rosemary L.; Wagstaff, Fred J.; Welch, Bruce L. 1992. Winter nutrient content and deer use of Gambel oak twigs in north central Utah. Great Basin Naturalist. 52:293-299.

Riggs, Robert A.; Urness, Phillip J. 1989. Effects of goat browsing on Gambel oak communities in northern Utah. Journal of Range Management. 42:354-360.

Smith, Arthur D.; Hubbard, Richard L. 1954. Preference ratings for winter deer forages from northern Utah ranges based on browsing time and forage consumed. Journal of Range Management. 7:262-265.

Sweeney, John R.; Sweeney, James M.; Steinhoff, Harold W. 1979. Effects of snow on browse production by Gambel oak. In: Swanson, Gustav A., tech. coord. The mitigation symposium: a national workshop on mitigating losses of fish and wildlife habitats; 1979 July 16-20; Fort Collins, CO. Gen. Tech. Rep. RM-65. Fort Collins, CO: U.S. Department of Agriculture, Forest Service, Rocky Mountain Forest and Range Experiment Station: 637-638.

Wolters, Gale L. 1996. Elk effects on Bandelier National Monument meadows and grasslands. In: Allen, Craig D., tech. ed. Fire effects in southwestern forests: proceedings of the second La Mesa Fire symposium; 1994 March 29-31; Los Alamos, NM. Gen. Tech. Rep. RM-GTR-286. Fort Collins, CO: U.S. Department of Agriculture, Forest Service, Rocky Mountain Forest and Range Experiment Station: 196-205.

9. Fire Regimes in Gambel Oak Communities

Baisan, Christopher H.; Swetnam, Thomas W. 1990. Fire history on a desert mountain range: Rincon Mountain Wilderness, Arizona, U.S.A. Canadian Journal of Forest Research. 20:1559-1569.

Floyd, M. Lisa; Romme, William H.; Hanna, David D. 2000. Fire history and vegetation pattern in Mesa Verde National Park, Colorado, USA. Ecological Applications. 10:1666-1680.

Fulé, Peter Z.; Crouse, Joseph E.; Heinlein, Thomas A.; Moore, Margaret M.; Covington, W. Wallace; Verkamp, Greg. 2003. Mixed-severity fire regime in a high-elevation forest: Grand Canyon, Arizona. Landscape Ecology. 18:465-486.

Fulé, Peter Z.; Heinlein, Thomas A.; Covington, W. Wallace; Moore, Margaret M. 2003. Assessing fire regimes on Grand Canyon landscapes with fire scar and fire record data. International Journal of Wildland Fire. 12:129-145.

Grissino-Mayer, Henri D.; Romme, William H.; Floyd, M. Lisa; Hanna, David D. 2004. Climatic and human influences on fire regimes of the southern San Juan Mountains, Colorado, USA. Ecology. 85:1708-1724.

Madany, Michael H.; West, Neil E. 1980. Fire history of two montane forest areas of Zion National Park. In: Stokes, Marvin H.; Dieterich, John H, tech. coords. Proceedings of the fire history workshop; 1980 October 20-24; Tucson, AZ. Gen. Tech. Rep. RM-81. Fort Collins, CO: U.S. Department of Agriculture, Forest Service, Rocky Mountain Forest and Range Experiment Station: 50-56.

Swetnam, Thomas W.; Dieterich, John H. 1985. Fire history of ponderosa pine forests in the Gila Wilderness, New Mexico. In: Lotan, James E.; Kilgore, B.M.; Fischer, W.C.; Mutch R.W., tech. coords. Proceedings—symposium and workshop on wilderness fire: 1983 November 15-18; Missoula, MT. Gen. Tech. Rep. INT-182. Ogden, UT: U.S. Department of Agriculture, Forest Service, Intermountain Forest and Range Experiment Station: 390-397.

Wadleigh, Linda L.; Parker, Carolie; Smith, Barbara. 1998. A fire frequency and comparative fuel load analysis in Gambel oak of northern Utah. In: Pruden, T.L.; Brennan, L.A., eds. Fire in ecosystem management: shifting the paradigm from suppression to prescription: 1996 May 7-10; Boise, ID. Tall Timbers Fire Ecology Conference Proceedings No. 20. Tallahassee, FL: Tall Timbers Research Station: 267-272.

10. Density and Vegetational Changes

Abella, Scott R.; Fulé, Peter Z. 2008. Changes in Gambel oak densities in southwestern ponderosa pine forests since Euro-American settlement. Res. Note RMRS-RN-36. Fort Collins, CO: U.S. Department of Agriculture, Forest Service, Rocky Mountain Research Station. 6 p.

Austin, Dennis D.; Urness, Philip J.; Riggs, Robert A. 1986. Vegetal changes in the absence of livestock grazing, mountain brush zone, Utah. Journal of Range Management. 39:514-517.

Christensen, Earl M. 1958. Growth rates and vegetation change in the oak-maple brush in lower Provo Canyon, Utah. Utah Academy of Sciences, Arts and Letters Proceedings. 35:167-168.

Covington, W. Wallace; Moore, Margaret M. 1994. Southwestern ponderosa forest structure: changes since Euro-American settlement. Journal of Forestry. 92:39-47.

Eastmond, Robert J. 1968. Vegetational changes in a mountain brush community of Utah during eighteen years. Provo, UT: Brigham Young University. 64 p. Thesis.

Floyd, Mary E. 1982. The interaction of piñon pine and Gambel oak in plant succession near Dolores, Colorado. Southwestern Naturalist. 27:143-147.

Fulé, Peter Z.; Covington, W. Wallace; Moore, Margaret M. 1997. Determining reference conditions for ecosystem management of southwestern ponderosa pine forests. Ecological Applications. 7:895-908.

Fulé, Peter Z.; Covington, W. Wallace; Moore, Marget M.; Heinlein, Thomas A.; Waltz, Amy E.M. 2002. Natural variability in forests of the Grand Canyon, USA. Journal of Biogeography. 29:31-47.

Fulé, Peter Z.; Covington, W. Wallace; Smith, H.B.; Springer, Judith D.; Heinlein, Thomas A.; Huisinga, Kristin D.; Moore, Margaret M. 2002. Comparing ecological restoration alternatives: Grand Canyon, Arizona. Forest Ecology and Management. 170:19-41.

Heinlein, Thomas A.; Covington, W. Wallace; Fulé, Peter Z.; Moore, Margaret M.; Smith, Hiram B. 2000. Development of ecological restoration experiments in fire adapted forests at Grand Canyon

USDA Forest Service Gen. Tech. Rep. RMRS-GTR-218. 2008

25

National Park. In: Cole, David N.; McCool, Stephen F.; Borrie, William T.; O'Loughlin, Jennifer, comps. Wilderness science in a time of change conference – volume 5: wilderness ecosystems, threats, and management; 1999 May 23-27; Missoula, MT. Proceedings RMRS-P-15-VOL-5. Ogden, UT: U.S. Department of Agriculture, Forest Service, Rocky Mountain Research Station: 249-254.

Madany, Michael H.; West, Neil E. 1983. Livestock grazing-fire regime interactions within montane forests of Zion National Park, Utah. Ecology. 64:661-667.

Medina, Alvin L.; Martin, S. Clark. 1988. Stream channel and vegetation changes in sections of McKnight Creek, New Mexico. Great Basin Naturalist. 48:373-381.

Menzel, Jody P.; Covington, W. Wallace. 1997. Changes from 1876 to 1994 in a forest ecosystem near Walnut Canyon, northern Arizona. In: van Ripler, Charles; Deshler, Elena T., eds. Proceedings of the third biennial conference of research on the Colorado Plateau; 1995; Flagstaff, AZ. Transactions and proceedings series NPS/NRNAU/NRTP-97/12, U.S. Department of the Interior, National Park Service: 151-172.

Ruess, Bradley J. 1995. Changes in Mexican spotted owl habitat within ponderosa pine/Gambel oak communities since Euro-American settlement. Flagstaff, AZ: Northern Arizona University. 42 p. Thesis.

Schuhardt, Susan. 1991. Structure, productivity, and competition in a ponderosa pine/Arizona white oak community. Flagstaff, AZ: Northern Arizona University. 119 p. Thesis.

Waltz, Amy E.M.; Fulé, Peter Z.; Covington, W. Wallace; Moore, Margaret M. 2003. Diversity in ponderosa pine forest structure following ecological restoration treatments. Forest Science. 49:885-900.

11. Responses to Management and Disturbance

Abella, Scott R.; Fulé, Peter Z. 2008. Fire effects on Gambel oak in southwestern ponderosa pine-oak forests. Res. Note RMRS-RN-34. Fort Collins, CO: U.S. Department of Agriculture, Forest Service, Rocky Mountain Research Station. 6 p.

Bowns, James E. 1985. Rehabilitation and management of Gambel oak (*Quercus gambelii*) dominated ranges in southwestern Utah. In: Johnson, Kendall L., ed. Proceedings of the Third Utah Shrub Ecology Workshop; 1983 August 30-31; Provo, UT. Logan, UT: Utah State University: 29-32.

Bradley, Ann F.; Noste, Nonan V.; Fischer, William C. 1992. Fire ecology of forests and woodlands in Utah. Gen. Tech. Rep. INT-287. Ogden, UT: U.S. Department of Agriculture, Forest Service, Intermountain Research Station. 128 p.

Brown, James K.; Smith, Jane Kapler, eds. 2000. Wildland fire in ecosystems: effects of fire on flora. Gen. Tech. Rep. RMRS-GTR-42-vol. 2. Ogden, UT: U.S. Department of Agriculture, Forest Service, Rocky Mountain Research Station. 257 p.

Davis, Gary G.; Bartel, Lawrence E.; Cook, C. Wayne. 1975. Control of Gambel oak sprouts by goats. Journal of Range Management. 28:216-218.

Engle, David M.; Bonham, Charles D. 1980. Nonstructural carbohydrates in roots of Gambel oak sprouts following herbicide treatment. Journal of Range Management. 33:390-394.

Engle, D.M.; Bonham, C.D.; Bartel, L.E. 1983. Ecological characteristics and control of Gambel oak. Journal of Range Management. 36:363-365.

Ffolliott, Peter F.; Gottfried, Gerald J. 1991. Natural tree regeneration after clearcutting in Arizona's ponderosa pine forests: two long-term case studies. Res. Note RM-507. Fort Collins, CO: U.S. Department of Agriculture, Forest Service, Rocky Mountain Forest and Range Experiment Station. 6 p.

Foxx, Teralene S. 1996. Vegetation succession after the La Mesa fire at Bandelier National Monument. In: Allen, Craig D., tech. ed. Fire effects in southwestern forests: proceedings of the second La Mesa Fire symposium; 1994 March 29-31; Los Alamos, NM. Gen. Tech. Rep. RM-GTR-286. Fort Collins, CO: U.S. Department of Agriculture, Forest Service, Rocky Mountain Forest and Range Experiment Station: 47-69.

Fulé, Peter Z.; Laughlin, Daniel C.; Covington, W. Wallace. 2005. Pine-oak forest dynamics five years after ecological restoration treatments, Arizona, USA. Forest Ecology and Management. 218:129-145.

Harrington, M.G. 1985. The effects of spring, summer, and fall burning on Gambel oak in a southwestern ponderosa pine stand. Forest Science. 31:156-163.

Harrington, M.G. 1989. Gambel oak root carbohydrate response to spring, summer, and fall prescribed burning. Journal of Range Management. 42:504-507.

Johnsen, Thomas N.; Clary, Warren P.; Ffolliott, Peter F. 1969. Gambel oak control on the Beaver Creek pilot watershed in Arizona. Crops Research, ARS 34-104. U.S. Department of Agriculture, Agricultural Research Service. 8 p.

Johnsen, Thomas N.; Dalen, Raymond S. 1984. Controlling individual junipers and oaks with pelleted picloram. Journal of Range Management. 37:380-384.

Kufeld, Roland C. 1977. Improving Gambel oak ranges for elk and mule deer by spraying with 2,4,5-TP. Journal of Range Management. 30:53-57.

Kunzler, L.M.; Harper, K.T. 1980. Recovery of Gambel oak after fire in central Utah. Great Basin Naturalist. 40:127-130.

Lauver, Chris L.; Jameson, Donald A.; Rittenhouse, Larry R. 1989. Management strategies for Gambel oak communities. Rangelands. 11:213-216.

Marquiss, Robert W. 1972. Soil moisture, forage, and beef production benefits from Gambel oak control in southwestern Colorado. Journal of Range Management. 25:146-150.

Marquiss, Robert W. 1973. Gambel oak control studies in southwestern Colorado. Journal of Range Management. 26:57-58.

McKell, Cyrus M. 1950. A study of plant succession in the oak brush (*Quercus gambelii*) zone after fire. Salt Lake City, UT: University of Utah. 79 p. Thesis.

Onkonburi, Jeanmarie. 1999. Growth response of Gambel oak to thinning and burning: implications for ecological restoration. Flagstaff, AZ: Northern Arizona University. 129 p. Dissertation.

Poreda, Stephen F.; Wullstein, Leroy H. 1994. Vegetation recovery following fire in an oakbrush vegetation mosaic. Great Basin Naturalist. 54:380-383.

Randall-Parker, Tammy; Miller, Richard. 2002. Effects of prescribed fire in ponderosa pine on key wildlife habitat components: preliminary results and a method for monitoring. In: Laudenslayer, William F.; Shea, Patrick J.; Valentine, Bradley E.; Weatherspoon, Phillip; Lisle, Thomas E., tech. coords. Proceedings of the symposium on the ecology and management of dead wood in western forests; 1999 November 2-4; Reno, NV. Gen. Tech. Rep. PSW-GTR-181. Albany, CA: U.S. Department of Agriculture, Forest Service, Pacific Southwest Research Station: 823-834.

Roccaforte, John Paul. 2005. Monitoring landscape-scale forest structure and potential fire behavior changes following ponderosa pine restoration treatments. Flagstaff, AZ: Northern Arizona University. 102 p. Thesis.

Savage, Melissa; Mast, Joy Nystrom. 2005. How resilient are southwestern ponderosa pine forests after crown fires? Canadian Journal of Forest Research. 35:967-977.

Simonin, Kevin A. 2000. *Quercus gambelii*. In: Fire effects information system [online]. U.S. Department of Agriculture, Forest Service, Rocky Mountain Research Station, Fire Sciences Laboratory. Available: http://www.fs.fed.us/database/feis/ [2005, June 20].

Stevens, Richard; Davis, James N. 1985. Opportunities for improving forage production in the Gambel oak types of Utah. In: Johnson, Kendall L., ed. Proceedings of the Third Utah Shrub Ecology Workshop; 1983 August 30-31; Provo, UT. Logan, UT: Utah State University: 37-41.

Vallentine, John F.; Schwendiman, DeWayne. 1973. Spot treatment for Gambel oak control. Journal of Range Management. 26:382-383.

Van Epps, Gordon A. 1974. Control of Gambel oak with three herbicides. Journal of Range Management. 27:297-301.

Winward, A.H. 1985. Perspectives on Gambel oak management on national forests of the Intermountain Region. In: Johnson, Kendall L., ed. Proceedings of the Third Utah Shrub Ecology Workshop; 1983 August 30-31; Provo, UT. Logan, UT: Utah State University: 33-35.

Wright, Henry A. 1972. Shrub response to fire. In: McKell, Cyrus M.; Blaisdell, James P.; Goodin, Joe R., tech. eds. Wildland shrubs – their biology and utilization; 1971 July; Logan, UT. Gen. Tech. Rep. INT-1. Ogden, UT: U.S. Department of Agriculture, Forest Service, Intermountain Forest and Range Experiment Station: 204-217.

USDA Forest Service Gen. Tech. Rep. RMRS-GTR-218. 2008

27

The Rocky Mountain Research Station develops scientific information and technology to improve management, protection, and use of the forests and rangelands. Research is designed to meet the needs of the National Forest managers, Federal and State agencies, public and private organizations, academic institutions, industry, and individuals. Studies accelerate solutions to problems involving ecosystems, range, forests, water, recreation, fire, resource inventory, land reclamation, community sustainability, forest engineering technology, multiple use economics, wildlife and fish habitat, and forest insects and diseases. Studies are conducted cooperatively, and applications may be found worldwide.

Station Headquarters
Rocky Mountain Research Station
240 W. Prospect Road
Fort Collins, CO 80526
(970) 498-1100

Research Locations

Flagstaff, Arizona	Reno, Nevada
Fort Collins, Colorado	Albuquerque, New Mexico
Boise, Idaho	Rapid City, South Dakota
Moscow, Idaho	Logan, Utah
Bozeman, Montana	Ogden, Utah
Missoula, Montana	Provo, Utah